Understanding Maths Learning Difficulties

Understanding Maths Learning Difficulties

Dyscalculia, Dyslexia or Dyspraxia?

Judy Hornigold

 Open University Press

Open University Press
McGraw-Hill Education
8th Floor, 338 Euston Road
London
England
NW1 3BH

email: enquiries@openup.co.uk
world wide web: www.openup.co.uk

and Two Penn Plaza, New York, NY 10121-2289, USA

First published 2017

A catalogue record of this book is available from the British Library

ISBN-13: 978-0-335-26244-1
ISBN-10: 0-33-526244-9
eISBN: 978-0-335-26245-8

Library of Congress Cataloging-in-Publication Data
CIP data applied for

Typeset by Transforma Pvt. Ltd., Chennai, India

Printed and bound by CPI Group (UK) Ltd, Croydon, CR0 4YY

Praise for this book

"This book is a comprehensive overview of the connections between maths, learning difficulties in maths and dyscalculia, backed by extensive references to pertinent research. It balances this research with a wealth of pragmatic advice, all communicated in a very accessible style."

Steve Chinn, Visiting Professor, University of Derby, UK

"The strengths of this book lie in its very well organised chapter choices, which build into a very clear account of the author's view of this still little understood subject. They build up to describing the differential diagnoses and their impact on a pupil's maths development, whilst acknowledging co-occurrences across the separate impacts of dyslexia and dyspraxia which can create a profile of the specific learning difficulty: dyscalculia.

This book will be ideal for the student building up their knowledge about learning difficulties in maths, but also very useful for the experienced practitioner who wants to keep up to date. Every reference is followed up with suggestions for further reading around every fascinating point made.

I liked this book, speaking as an experienced dyscalculia specialist, as I learnt a lot, and felt hungry to follow up many points with further reading."

Jane Emerson, Numeracy Specialist Teacher and co-author of
The Dyscalculia Assessment, The Dyscalculia
Solution and Understanding Dyscalculia
and Numeracy Difficulties

"All children can learn maths; yet many fear it and fail. This book describes how problems arise from the way that maths is taught as well as from specific learning difficulties. It explains what goes wrong, and why, and offers solutions. Multi-sensory learning is the key to success: children develop

reasoning skills and conceptual understanding by discussing their thoughts as they manipulate objects. The final chapter has brilliant ideas to spark every child's curiosity so that even the most reluctant will want to learn."

Patricia Babtie, Dyscalculia teacher,
lecturer and author, London

For my boys, Thomas, James and Sam, and also for Alan, without whom I would never have completed this book on time. Thank you.

Contents

Maths difficulties

> Do not worry about your difficulties in mathematics. I can assure you mine are still greater.
>
> > Albert Einstein

Why do so many children find maths difficult?

Maths is one of the most important subjects taught in schools. Education systems around the world emphasize its status as a key subject and most employers expect applicants to have achieved a certain level in maths. Yet, it is the one subject that can strike fear and dread in children from the very start of their education. Professor Steve Chinn has researched the age at which teachers notice children giving up on maths. Alarmingly, he found this to be at 6 or 7 years of age, something that is unique to maths – children don't give up on any other subject at such a young age. So, is it the subject itself or is it the way that it is being taught? This chapter examines the demands of maths, to determine whether there are skills that are particular to maths that are causing such difficulties among young learners. Furthermore, it will examine the way that the subject is sometimes presented to children in an attempt to understand why children often decide, after a very short time, that maths is not for them.

Demands of maths

Success in maths requires a combination of skills and abilities. Joffe (1980) noted that children need strong visual and verbal abilities, and the means to integrate these skills, such as using mathematical language to describe and explain a mathematical diagram. They also need good spatial skills for understanding shape, symmetry, relative size and quantity, and good linear skills for understanding the sequential and ordered symbols and representations found in the number system and algebra.

Maths also requires the ability to:

- store, access, and retrieve information effectively;
- use working memory efficiently in terms of both capacity and time;
- combine creative thought with structured mental organization;
- process information quickly and accurately;
- learn, understand, and remember rules and procedures.

These are not skills that come easily to learners with specific learning difficulties, such as dyscalculia, dyslexia, and dyspraxia. It is hardly surprising, then, that many of these learners struggle with maths.

The purpose of this book is to explore the specific difficulties that learners with dyscalculia, dyslexia, and dyspraxia have with maths and will offer strategies to support these children. However, let us first put these internal factors to one side in order to explore the many external factors that can influence someone's ability in maths.

Around 25% of children in a class are likely to struggle with maths at some time in their lives. This percentage is much higher than the percentage of children with specific learning difficulties. Evidently, there must be external factors at work contributing to these difficulties. It may be that these children have not understood a fundamental concept, such as place value, which can have a huge impact on later learning. It is widely known that if you learn something incorrectly the first time that you encounter it, then it is very difficult to 'undo' that learning. This is because when you learn something new there is a physical connection of neurons, and this initial connection will want to become the default connection. If you have registered something incorrectly the first time, then you will have to suppress this neural pathway and train the brain to build a new pathway that has a stronger connection than the original one. This effect is sometimes paraphrased as 'neurons that fire together, wire together'. That is why it is so important that children are presented with a clear, unambiguous representation of new learning so that it is correctly registered the first time that they encounter it. When I was very young and learning my colour names, I got blue and red mixed up and to this day I sometimes see a blue top yet call it red!

The cumulative nature of maths can also cause problems, particularly in young children who are prone to illness and consequently can miss out on the teaching of a particular idea or concept. They may then find it difficult to catch up on their return. Subsequently, it can be very hard to build on these rocky foundations, leading to a perpetual feeling of not quite understanding what's going on.

The subject itself

Maths is a cumulative subject consisting of many different parts. Dowker (2004) stated that skill in arithmetic is not a single unitary ability at which people are either 'good' or 'bad'. Studies of children with mathematical difficulties (e.g. Butterworth and Yeo 2004; Geary and Hoard 2005) support this point of view.

There are many components to mathematical ability, including counting, memory for facts and procedures, reasoning and understanding of mathematical concepts. These components overlap and interconnect, so that a weakness in one can often impact on another. The complex nature of these components can result in a child having a problem in one area and then extrapolating this problem to the whole subject, perceiving that they are 'bad at maths' rather than just having difficulty with a certain aspect, such as recalling their times tables facts. Certain components are prerequisites to others and this is often where children first start to have difficulty with maths. One of the most common difficulties is place value, but for many children the problems start much earlier than this.

Early numerical development

We know that babies are born with an understanding of numerical quantity (Dehaene 2011). Research has shown that infants as young as 6 months can distinguish between a random array of 8 dots and one of 16 dots (Starkey and Cooper 1980). By the time they reach 9 months old they have refined this skill to be able to distinguish between 8 and 12 dots. However, this ability to assess numerical quantity appears to be missing in children with dyscalculia. They also have difficulty linking the representation of numerical quantity to our adopted cultural symbols for number. Children with dyscalculia find it hard to integrate a representation of a numerical quantity, say a set of 3 counters, to the symbol '3' (see Figure 1.1).

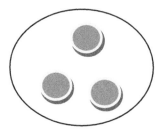

Figure 1.1 Representation of a numerical quantity

So the difficulty here is with accessing the meaning of the squiggle (3) that we call 'three'. This has been demonstrated using a number Stroop task (Butterworth et al. 2000). In this task, a group of dyscalculic children and a group of non-dyscalculic children were given two numbers to look at:

Congruent pair		Incongruent pair		Neutral pair/ numerical task		Neutral pair/ physical task	
3	5	5	3	3	5	3	3

In the congruent pair, the numerically larger number is also physically larger. In the incongruent pair, the numerically larger number is physically smaller. The incongruent pair shows the Stroop effect. Here, the child has to access the numerical value of the number and suppress the physical size of the number.

When the children were asked to identify which number was physically larger, there was no difference in response time between the dyscalculic and non-dyscalculic group. However, when asked to identify which was the numerically larger number, there was a marked difference between the two groups. The dyscalculic children found it much harder to access the meaning of the numerical symbol. Price et al. (2007) have carried out research indicating that dyscalculia is a more generalized magnitude-processing problem, where it is difficult to distinguish the length of rods or even the intensity of tones. Therefore, it can be seen as a spatial difficulty.

The ability to process numerical magnitude is often referred to as the *approximate number system*. We use this ability to approximate numerical quantities, such as deciding which is the shorter queue at the supermarket checkout. As evidenced, a crucial step in early numerical development is being able to understand numerical quantity in concrete, pictorial, and abstract form. In other words, looking at a set of three teddies and knowing that the symbol 3 stands for that quantity and also knowing how that quantity, 3, relates to other numerical quantities: 3 teddies are less than 5 teddies but more than 1 teddy. This understanding of numerical quantity is an important predictor of future mathematical ability. It links to the *object tracking system*, which is our ability to instantaneously and precisely determine the value of a set of up to four objects (Piazza et al. 2011). This is also referred to as subitizing. Dyscalculic learners experience difficulty with both the object tracking system and the approximate number system. They do not have the ability to subitize even small sets of objects and also find it hard to compare the magnitudes of numbers. When presented with a bowl of three apples, dyscalculic learners may need to count the apples rather than just immediately comprehending that the quantity is three. When presented with two digits, say 9 and 5, they may not be able to ascertain which digit represents the larger number.

Finger representations

Dyscalculic learners find it difficult to achieve early numerical developmental milestones as illustrated above, and research now suggests that finger representation ability can also be a reliable predictor of future mathematical ability. Many children are given the impression that it is babyish and 'wrong' to use your fingers when doing maths. However, there is a great deal of research that supports and actively encourages finger use. It is a vital stage of mathematical development and also a predictor of future mathematical success. Berteletti and Booth (2015) have studied the somatosensory finger area of the brain, an area of the brain that 'sees' fingers. This part of the brain is activated even when we are at an age when we have stopped using our fingers to count. It is the somatosensory finger area of the brain that is responsible for the perception and representation of fingers. Research using MRI scanning has shown that the somatosensory finger area lights up when we undertake a mathematical task, showing that our brains are wired up to use our fingers when doing maths. By telling children that they should not use their fingers, we are suppressing a natural reaction. It has also been shown that good finger representation is a useful predictor of later mathematical ability. Thus, if at an early age you can identify which of your fingers another person is touching, without looking, you have good finger representation. Finger representation can be developed through training, an example of which would be to apply coloured dots to the finger nails and then carrying out activities that require matching fingers to specific colours.

Butterworth (1999), a leading researcher in this area, believes that children need to learn about number through thinking about their fingers and if they are not given the opportunity to do so, then numbers will never have a 'normal representation' in the brain. Boaler and Chen (2016) concur with this view, commenting, 'Stopping students from using their fingers when they count could be akin to halting their mathematical development. Fingers are probably one of our most useful visual aids, and the finger area of our brain is used well into adulthood.'

Activities for developing finger discrimination are provided in Chapter 9.

Counting: as easy as 1, 2, 3?

Learning to count is a lot trickier than it looks. Children engage in oral counting from a very early age, but there are many different levels of this 'oral counting'.

The first level, according to Fuson (1988), is the *string* level, when the child perceives the counting words as a continuous sound string: 'onetwothreefour . . .'. Later on, the child will progress to the *unbreakable list* level, when he or she is able to appreciate that the counting sequence is comprised of separate words. This is referred to as the unbreakable list level because the child will always start with one and will not be able to break the sequence. Progression from this leads to the *breakable chain* level, where the child will learn to start from any point in the sequence, meaning they won't have to start counting from one. This is essential for calculation skills such as counting on.

For most children, the next stage will be the *bi-directional* level, where they can say the numbers both forwards and backwards and starting from any point in the sequence. A more advanced level is the *numerable chain* level. Now the child can start counting from any point and has learned to appreciate the difference between ordinal and cardinal numbers.

So, we can see that counting is much more complex than just reciting the numbers from 1 to 10. Gelman and Gallistel (1986) identified a set of counting principles that children need to understand if they are to truly understand our counting system. These can be described as follows:

> **Stable order principle:** Understanding that the counting sequence remains consistent. It is always 1, 2, 3, 4, 5, 6, 7, 8, 9, 10, etc., not 1, 2, 4, 5, 8, 3, 9, 10, 6, 7 say.
>
> **Order irrelevance principle:** Understanding that the counting of objects can begin with any object in a set and the total will stay the same.
>
> **One-to-one correspondence principle:** Understanding that each object being counted must be given one count and only one count.
>
> **Cardinality principle:** Understanding that the last count of a group of objects represents how many are in the group. A child who re-counts when asked how many sweets there are in the set that they have just counted has not understood the cardinality principle.
>
> **Conservation principle:** Understanding that the count for a set group of objects stays the same no matter whether they are spread out or close together.
>
> **Abstraction principle:** Understanding that the quantity of five large things is the same count as a quantity of five small things. Or the quantity is the same as a mixed group of five small, medium, and large things. Young children who have not acquired this counting principle will often think that a set of 3 elephants is numerically larger than a set of 3 mice.
>
> **Movement is magnitude principle:** Understanding that as you move up the counting sequence, the quantity increases by one and as you move down or backwards, the quantity decreases by one (or by whatever number you are counting by – in skip counting by 10's, the amount goes up by 10 each time).

Unitizing principle: Understanding that in our base ten system objects are grouped into tens when the count exceeds 9 and that this is indicated by a 1 in the tens place of a number.

Often, due to the demands of the curriculum, teachers have to move through these early counting experiences too quickly and this can leave some children with an incomplete understanding of these number concepts and principles.

Place value

Another common area of difficulty is place value. Many children have difficulty understanding place value, particularly when they are subtracting with decomposition. For example, to subtract 19 from 43 you need to exchange one of the tens for ten ones. Children who aren't secure with place value may often calculate 43 – 19 as 36, because they have ignored place value and have just taken 1 from 4 in the tens column and then 3 from 9 in the ones column. This sort of error stems from the misuse of the earlier subtraction strategy of 'taking away the smaller number from the larger number'. Koshy et al. (1999) identified that children make more mistakes with subtraction than any other operation.

One way to support children with place value is to make sure that they have access to appropriate manipulatives. Base ten materials, formerly known as Dienes materials after their inventor, Zoltan Dienes, are ideal for this purpose and are very effective at showing the value of numbers. As shown in Figure 1.2, cubes are used to represent one, rods to represent ten, flats to represent 100, and blocks to represent 1,000. The children can physically see that 10 cubes make one 'ten' rod, 10 rods make one 'hundred' flat, and 10 flats make the 1,000 block.

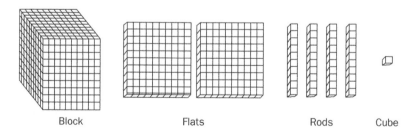

Block   Flats   Rods   Cube

Figure 1.2 Base ten materials

Bruner (1960) proposed that children need to go through three distinct stages if they are to fully understand a mathematical concept. These stages are enactive (concrete), iconic (pictorial), and symbolic (abstract). Briefly, his model can be described as follows. At the *concrete* level manipulatives are used to physically explore and solve problems. Then, at the *pictorial* level pictures, drawings, diagrams, charts, and graphs are used as visual representations of the concrete manipulatives. Finally, at the *abstract* level symbolic representations are used to represent and solve the problem.

When children are trying to understand place value, it is important that enough time is spent on the concrete and pictorial stages. The prolonged and consistent use of base ten materials can help children to understand when they need to exchange and when they don't. It helps them to make sense of the mathematical algorithm.

Without a sound understanding of place value, children will not be able to perform mental and written calculations effectively. They need to go through the following steps, in depth and with the support of concrete manipulatives in order to gain a robust understanding of place value.

1   Understanding that the symbol 1 can represent one ten as well as one unit, depending on its place in a number.
2   Understanding that you can have numbers that are made up of tens and ones. For example, 21 is a number made up from two tens and one unit.
3   Matching number names to number symbols. For example, understanding that we call the number 'one ten and two units', twelve.
4   Understanding that 10 tens make one hundred and that this is represented in a different place from the tens and the ones.
5   Developing flexibility and number sense when working with number. For example, 54 is 5 tens and 4 ones, but it is also 3 tens and 24 ones.
6   Generalizing their knowledge of place value to being able to understand and correctly represent hundreds, thousands, and tens of thousands.

For many children, misconceptions around these early mathematical concepts can persist into adulthood and can pose a real barrier to learning in maths.

The pedagogy of maths

The methods employed in teaching maths can also be instrumental in causing difficulties for children. Greenwood (1984: 662–3) commented, 'Evidence suggests that math anxiety results more from the way the subject is presented than from the subject itself.' Jo Boaler, Professor of Education at Stanford University and author of *The Elephant in the Classroom*, has identified, from her extensive research, three main areas that she feels are implicated in the problems that young children have in acquiring mathematical competence. First, she feels that children have a much too narrow experience of maths, with too much emphasis on reproducing methods that have been demonstrated by the teacher. This can be very demotivating for children, who have no ownership over their learning and can lead them to wonder what the point of it all really is. This approach can also lead to higher levels of maths anxiety. Since they don't have a grasp of the underlying concepts, the children have no option but to rely on remembering procedures and learning facts by rote.

Second, she feels that children are presented with 'too much too early'. Mathematical content is 'frontloaded' in the early years. There has been a belief that speed is of the essence in maths. The faster we can answer and the faster that we can race through the curriculum, the better. Happily, the new National Curriculum emphasizes depth rather than acceleration, and this is a very welcome change of emphasis for children and teachers alike.

> Pupils who grasp concepts rapidly should be challenged through being offered rich and sophisticated problems before any acceleration through new content. Those who are not sufficiently fluent with earlier material should consolidate their understanding, including through additional practice, before moving on.
>
> (DfE 2014: 1)

Boaler also points out that ability grouping in mathematics can lead children to believe that they are 'no good at mathematics' from a very early age. Many children will conform to the expectations that we place on them and so if they are put into sets in line with their perceived ability, they will match their level of attainment accordingly. Streaming is nonsensical, in maths in particular, as it is such a diverse subject. Finding one area of maths challenging does not mean that you will find all areas of maths equally as challenging. Boaler advocates mixed ability groups, and also supports presenting children with 'low-threshold/high-ceiling tasks'. These tasks are easy for every child to access but hard to complete in full. Tasks like this allow the more able children to explore the concept in greater depth. Boaler also advocates the promotion of a 'growth mindset' in mathematics. This follows on from the work of Dweck (2006), who focused on how differing attitudes affect the way that people view both themselves and their interactions with others. She argues that there are two fundamental mindsets that people use: the fixed mindset and the growth mindset. Boaler (2013) relates the concept of a growth mindset to the teaching of maths. She suggests that these two opposing beliefs have huge implications for learning. Those with a growth mindset are persistent, learn from their mistakes, and are encouraged by other people's success. Those with a fixed mindset hate to fail because they believe that this tells them that they are bad at maths and consequently they avoid challenges in maths at all costs.

This has implications for the dyscalculic learner, as adopting a growth mindset will encourage them to persist and will give them the belief that they can develop their mathematical ability. The concept of growth mindset is explored in more detail in Chapter 8.

Misunderstanding what maths is really all about

The teaching of mathematics is all too often focused around using the tools of the trade rather than investigating what these tools can be used for. You can teach someone how to use a hammer, nails and wood, and they can happily hammer away for hours on end, but the whole endeavour will be pointless unless you show them the wonderful things that they can make. Marcus du Sautoy (2008), in an article for the *Guardian* newspaper, eloquently summed this up: 'Being a good speller does not make you a good writer, being a good calculator does not make you a good mathematician.'

Over the years, maths teaching has tended to become too compartmentalized. Topics are taught discretely and children are encouraged to become proficient in using procedures at speed, regardless of whether they understand the mathematical concepts that underlie them. The results-orientated focus is not conducive to embracing a problem-solving, concept-led approach to the teaching of maths.

Teachers often feel constrained to follow a curriculum that rewards speed and accuracy above all else, at the expense of creativity, collaboration or curiosity. For children with specific learning difficulties, this only serves to make the world of mathematics even more abstract and meaningless.

Boaler (2009) has described the maths that is taught in schools as 'fake mathematics', and claims that there is a huge gap between this and 'real mathematics', a gap that we urgently need to bridge. It seems that there is a significant mismatch between the way that we teach mathematics and the way that children learn mathematics. Rawson (1984) offered the following advice on the teaching of mathematics: 'Teach the subject as it is to the child as he is.'

This mismatch appears to be based on a fundamental misunderstanding of what mathematics actually is. Devlin (2000: 7) states that: 'Mathematics is not about numbers, but about life. It is about the world in which we live. It is about ideas. And far from being dull and sterile, as it is so often portrayed, it is full of creativity.' Chinn (2012) reiterated this mismatch between teaching and learning by suggesting that 'there is a need to take an approach to teaching mathematics that is more cognisant of how pupils learn partly by using our knowledge of why children with special needs do not learn to inform how we teach all of our children'.

Historically there has been too much focus on being correct and too little focus on being prepared to conjecture and to make mistakes. Children's anxiety around mathematics is only heightened by this obsession with accuracy. Instead, we should be developing a culture in mathematics that embraces, and learns from, mistakes. Such a culture would enable dyscalculic learners to explore the subject in a way that is meaningful to them.

Timed activities

There is a perception in mathematics that time is of the essence: the quicker you can answer, the better a mathematician you are. However, this depends on your view as to what exactly maths is all about. If you believe that maths is about calculations, then it would be an advantage to be able to do them quickly. However, if you believe that maths is more to do with how we approach and solve problems, then speed is not of the essence. The way that we think and the ideas that we have are of more importance and these can take time.

The following quote is from Laurent Schwartz, a French mathematician. In 1950 he was awarded the Fields Medal, the highest honour in maths, much like a Nobel Prize.

> I was always deeply uncertain about my own intellectual capacity; I thought I was unintelligent and it is true that I was, and still am, rather slow. I need time to seize things because I always need to understand them fully. Towards the end of the eleventh grade, I secretly thought of myself as stupid. I worried about this for a long time. I'm still just as slow . . . At the end of the eleventh grade, I took the measure of the situation, and came to the conclusion that rapidity doesn't have a precise relation to intelligence. What is important is to deeply understand things and their relations to each other. This is where intelligence lies. The fact of being quick or slow isn't really relevant.
>
> (Schwartz 2001: 30)

In the National Council of Teachers of Mathematics publication *Teaching Children Mathematics*, Boaler (2014: 470) comments that: 'In too many math classrooms, students believe that their role is to *perform* – to show they know math and can answer questions correctly – rather than to learn' (emphasis in original). Furthermore, Engle (2002, cited in Boaler 2014: 469) reported that 'researchers now know that students experience stress on timed tests that they do not experience even when working on the same math questions in untimed conditions'.

So, it is clear that performing maths tasks under time pressure is contributing to the anxiety felt by many children in maths lessons and is not helping them to develop their enjoyment and understanding of the subject.

The *right* answer

Many children feel anxious because they perceive maths as a subject where there is a right and a wrong answer. Although it is certainly true that some problems have a unique correct answer, for example $6 \times 7 = 42$, this is not the case for the vast majority of mathematical problems. It is simply that we are only teaching children the areas of maths that are focused on correct calculation.

Technological advances mean that we don't need to be expert calculators any more – we have machines to do the calculating for us.

The skill that we need now is to understand the concepts in maths that will help us to solve the problems that we are likely to meet in the workplace and in our everyday lives. No employer is going to be impressed with an applicant who can recite their tables in any order at breakneck speed! That is little more than a feat of memory. What they will be impressed with is someone who can draw on their knowledge and understanding of maths to formulate a solution to a problem, someone who can make decisions based on the calculations performed by computers.

Unfortunately, we have a system that remains focused on calculation – it is easier to quantify in terms of marking and grading. You have either got it right or wrong. No subjectivity and no margin for misinterpretation. Devlin (2014) illustrates this point beautifully. He states: 'Broadly speaking, mathematical thinking is a way of approaching problems that is based on classical mathematics, but takes account of the fact that computation (both numeric and symbolic) can be readily done by machines.' In practical terms, what this means is that people can now focus all their attention on real-world problems in the form they are encountered. Knowing how to solve an equation is no longer a valuable human ability; what matters now is formulating the equation to solve that problem in the first place, and then taking the result of the machine solution to the equation and making use of it.

I frequently hear teachers lamenting that we are not producing mathematicians in schools, only children who can get to a certain arbitrary level and all too often we are teaching to the tests rather than teaching the subject as it is in all its curious glory. If we focus solely on the right answer, then we not only lose the true essence of maths but also many of the its interesting and creative aspects.

In her article 'What's right about looking at what's wrong?', Deborah Schifter (2007: 22) asserted that 'both students and teachers gain new mathematical understanding by examining the reasoning behind a child's incorrect answer'. Knowing that a child has an incorrect answer tells us very little; the valuable information comes from exploring how the child arrived at that answer. The beauty and richness in mathematics comes from exploration and investigation, where mistakes are valued as positive learning experiences. We need to move away from a culture that focuses on procedure and fact recall to one that values creativity and deep conceptual understanding.

However, this approach to mathematics requires a deep level of understanding on the part of the teacher and the confidence to teach mathematics in a more conceptual way. Many teachers themselves have been taught mathematics as a set of discrete procedures and rules to be memorized, so there is a significant challenge in enabling them to implement a more collaborative and inquisitive approach to mathematics teaching. Williams' Independent Review of Mathematics Teaching (2008), produced by the Department for Children, Schools and Families in the UK, singled out two key issues: first, the need for an increased focus on the 'use and application' of mathematics and second, the vital importance of classroom discussion of mathematics. The review highlighted that constructive dialogue in the classroom was essential for fully developing mathematical logic and reasoning.

Another area of concern in the pedagogy of mathematics is that too many lessons focus on answering questions. Peter Hilton, an algebraic topologist, turns this idea on its head by suggesting that the essence of mathematics is inherently about being able to come up with the questions not answers. His view is that computation involves going from a question to an answer, whereas maths involves going from an answer to a question (cited by Boaler 2009). Such an approach would make mathematics lessons much more creative and would also make them more inclusive for the child with dyscalculia.

Boaler (2009) asserts that children need to be given the opportunity to ask their own questions to bring maths to life. Moreover, that there is a need to move away from the notion that all the maths in the world has previously been discovered and all that children need to do is to learn it. In her book *'The Having of Wonderful Ideas' and Other Essays on Teaching and Learning*, Duckworth (1996) makes the point that the most valuable learning experiences come from your own thoughts and ideas. We need to encourage this in mathematics as much, if not more, than in any other subject and let the children discover the maths for themselves.

Competition among children

Some children thrive on competition and it definitely has its place in education, but for children who lack confidence in maths, the element of competition only helps to reinforce their insecurities and anxieties. It is far better to work on a child's mindset in maths and to encourage them to compete against themselves rather than against each other.

Working in isolation

Vygotsky (1978) argued that social interaction was a vital component of problem-solving in maths and children's understanding would deepen through such interactions. This makes sense, as children are exposed to different ideas and different ways of thinking, enabling them to explore and test out a variety of solutions. He stated that social activity would promote intellectual development.

Mercer and Sams carried out research in this area, using an intervention called 'Thinking together', and concluded that 'children can be enabled to use talk more effectively as a tool for reasoning; and that talk-based group activities can help the development of individuals' mathematical reasoning, understanding and problem-solving' (2006: 507). Yet, many maths lessons focus on individuals working alone and this can be an added cause of anxiety leading to a lack of progress in many children.

Memorization rather than understanding

For many children maths becomes a list of facts and procedures that have to be learned. I remember being taught how to divide a fraction by another fraction. We just learned to change the divide to a multiply and then invert the second fraction. Some of us will remember this as:

Ours is not to reason why just invert and multiply.

Many schools today teach this method as 'keep, change, flip'. None of the above does anything to promote understanding and if you forget the rule, or remember it incorrectly, then you have nowhere to turn to, and no way of working out the answer. Sharma (1987: 8) identified the three components in a mathematical idea. He stated that 'Almost every mathematics idea, except simple arithmetic facts, consists of three components: linguistic, conceptual and skill/procedural.' Sharma went on to explain that by focusing on the procedural rather than the concept and language, children will have an insufficient understanding of the mathematical idea. They won't be able to work fully with that idea, or to generalize the idea to other scenarios. The implication of this model of a mathematical idea is clear – there should be equal emphasis on all three components when teaching maths, not on the procedural element alone.

Context

The context in which the question is asked can also make a huge difference to how a child may understand and approach that question. Far too often, maths problems are presented in isolation, devoid of any context. For example:

> Calculate 2003 – 1996

Some children may use a column subtraction method, which is tricky as they will have to deal with the zeros. However, we can make this problem more accessible by adding context, saying:

> If I was born in 1996, how old was I in 2003?

A child is much more likely to count up to 2000 and then add on 3, to give the answer 7. This is a much more sensible approach than using the column method of subtraction.

Similarly, children should be encouraged to contextualize maths questions by thinking about what the numbers could relate to in real life. So if we were adding 362 to 178, encourage the children to think what we could have 362 of and why we would be adding 178. This also helps the children to appreciate the magnitude of a number. It is not realistic to think that in this problem we are talking about brothers and sisters, for example. No-one has 362 brothers and 178 sisters. However, we could be saying that there are 362 children in the playground and 178 children in the dinner hall. How many children are there altogether?

By setting a problem in context we are demonstrating to the children that there is a reason why we need to solve the problem. It also helps them to visualize the maths and stops it from being just an abstract meaningless calculation.

Cultural attitudes to maths

Mathematics has the unique and unenviable status of being a subject that many are happy to admit being bad at. Whereas one would not dream of saying 'I can't do English', it is socially acceptable and in some cases seen as a badge of honour to be bad at mathematics. The media can also contribute to this attitude, as evidenced by a recent advert for a large supermarket. The advert was promoting half price school uniforms, as part of their back-to-school campaign. The wording was along the lines of: the 'good news is that school uniform is half price, the bad news is that the first lesson back at school is double maths!'

Sometimes, and often unwittingly, parents can also convey their own negative perceptions of maths to their children. I often hear parents saying, 'I am no good at maths' in front of their children and this can perpetuate the impression that maths is a difficult subject and that it is acceptable not to be good at it. Children pick up on this very early on and see maths as a hard subject, and sometimes as a subject that only boys are good at. Yet, being numerate is a life skill that we all need and the effects of innumeracy can be devastating. Butterworth and Yeo (2004) found that people with poor numeracy skills were more likely to be unemployed, depressed or ill. Parsons and Bynner (2005) noted that around 20% of the UK population have difficulties with mathematics that result in significant practical, educational or functional difficulties. The implications are not only social; Gross et al. (2009) reported that innumeracy among adults costs the UK exchequer as much as £2.4 billion every year.

So how can we change this perception and turn maths into a 'cool' subject? Clearly this won't happen overnight, but it is possible to change attitudes to a subject. Physics used to be seen as very 'geeky' but the 'Brian Cox effect' and TV programmes like 'The Big Bang Theory' have worked their magic and attitudes towards physics have changed dramatically over the past ten years. The numbers of students applying to study physics at Manchester University (where Brian Cox lectures) have increased to such an extent that the University now requires 2 A*s and an A at 'A' level. This is higher than the grades required for both Oxford and Cambridge.

There are several mathematicians in the media who are making great inroads into our cultural attitudes to maths and who are expertly showing the beauty, wonder, and everyday relevance of maths.

Marcus du Sautoy

Marcus du Sautoy is the Charles Simonyi Professor for the Public Understanding of Science at Oxford University. He is also a Professor of Mathematics and a Fellow of New College. He has made numerous programmes for television and writes for *The Times*, *The Daily Telegraph*, *The Independent*, and *The Guardian* and is frequently asked for comment on BBC radio and television. His TV shows include 'The School of Hard Sums' presented with Dara O'Briain, which is a light-hearted battle to solve mathematical conundrums. In 2011, he made a landmark documentary series called 'The Code', in which viewers were taken on an odyssey to reveal that mathematics is the hidden code at work in the world. A couple of his many books that I would recommend are: *The Number Mysteries* (2011), based on the Royal Institution Christmas Lectures of 2006 exploring some of the greatest unsolved problems of mathematics, and *The Music of the Primes* (2003), which presents the story of those who have tried to capture one of the greatest unsolved problems of mathematics, the pattern of prime numbers.

Alex Bellos

Alex Bellos has written two of my favourite books of all time, *Alex's Adventures in Numberland* (2011) and *Alex Through the Looking Glass* (2014). In these books, Alex travels the world interviewing people whose lives are connected to maths in some way. They are both highly entertaining, fascinating, and require no expert knowledge of maths at all. Alex has also contributed the most viewed Numberphile YouTube clip, a way of cutting a cake that he had written about in *Alex's Adventures in Numberland* (find it at www.youtube.com/watch?v=wBU9N35ZHIw).

Hannah Fry

Hannah Fry is a lecturer in the Mathematics of Cities at the Centre for Advanced Spatial Analysis at University College, London. She studies the patterns in human behaviour, particularly in an urban setting. Her research applies to a wide range of social problems and questions, from shopping and transport to urban crime, riots, and terrorism. Hannah has made several BBC documentaries including 'Climate Change by Numbers', 'Calculating Ada: The Countess of Computing' (BBC4), and 'Horizon: How to Find Love Online' (BBC2). Online, her YouTube videos have over 5 million views, including her popular TED talk, 'The Mathematics of Love'.

She describes the book of the same name (Fry 2015) that followed the TED talk as follows:

> I'll be the first to admit that love and mathematics don't seem to fit naturally together. I know – just as well as you do – that the thrill of romance can't easily be described by a simple set of equations. But that doesn't mean that maths doesn't have anything to offer. And by picking out big questions that maths is ideally placed to describe, I hope to persuade you that maths can offer a valuable new perspective on matters of the heart: What's the chance of us finding love? What's the chance that it will last? How does online dating work, exactly? When should you settle down? How can you avoid divorce? When is it right to compromise? Can game theory help us decide whether or not to call?
>
> (www.hannahfry.co.uk/)

Interesting questions indeed!

So, there are many people championing maths in the media and beyond and hopefully this sea change will gain momentum and we can move to a society where we not only enjoy maths but thrive on it.

References

Bellos, A. (2011) *Alex's Adventures in Numberland*. London: Bloomsbury.

Bellos, A. (2014) *Alex Through the Looking Glass*. London: Bloomsbury.

Berteletti, I. and Booth, J.R. (2015) Perceiving fingers in single-digit arithmetic problems, *Frontiers in Psychology*, 6: 226 [DOI: 10.3389/fpsyg.2015.00226].

Boaler, J. (2009) *The Elephant in the Classroom*. London: Souvenir Press.

Boaler, J. (2013) Ability and mathematics: the mindset revolution that is reshaping education, *FORUM*, 55(1): 143–52.

Boaler, J. (2014) Research suggests that timed tests cause math anxiety, *Teaching Children Mathematics*, 20(8): 469–73.

Boaler, J. and Chen, L. (2016) Why kids should use their fingers in maths class, *The Atlantic* [retrieved from: https://www.theatlantic.com/education/archive/2016/04/why-kids-should-use-their-fingers-in-math-class/478053/; accessed 18 March 2017].

Bruner, J.S. (1960) *The Process of Education*. Cambridge, MA: Harvard University Press.

Butterworth, B. (1999) *What Counts: How every brain is hardwired for maths*. New York: Free Press.

Butterworth, B. and Yeo, D. (2004) *Dyscalculia Guidance: Helping Pupils with Specific Learning Difficulties in Maths*. London: NFER/Nelson.

Butterworth, B., Girelli, L. and Lucangeli, D. (2000) The development of automaticity in accessing number magnitude, *Journal of Experimental Child Psychology*, 76(2): 104–22.

Chinn, S. (2012) Keynote speech, First International Dyscalculia Conference, London.

Dehaene, S. (2011) *The Number Sense*. New York: Oxford University Press.

Department for Education (2014) *The National Curriculum in England: Key Stages 1 and 2 Framework Document* [retrieved from: https://www.gov.uk/government/publications/national-curriculum-in-england-primary-curriculum; accessed 18 March 2017].

Devlin, K. (2000) *The Math Gene: How mathematical thinking evolved and why numbers are like gossip*. New York: Basic Books.

Devlin, K. (2014) Most math problems do not have a unique right answer, *Devlin's Angle* [retrieved from: http://devlinsangle.blogspot.co.uk/2014/08/most-math-problems-do-not-have-unique.html; accessed 26 September 2016].

Dowker, A. (2004) *What Works for Children with Mathematical Difficulties?* Research Report #554. London: DfES.

Duckworth, E. (1996) *'The Having of Wonderful Ideas' and Other Essays on Teaching and Learning*. New York: Teacher's College Press.

du Sautoy, M. (2003) *The Music of the Primes*. London: Fourth Estate.

du Sautoy, M. (2008) 'I'm not very fast at my times tables', *The Guardian*, 3 November [retrieved from: https://www.theguardian.com/science/2008/nov/03/marcus-dusautoy; accessed 26 September 2016].

du Sautoy, M. (2011) *The Number Mysteries*. London: Fourth Estate.

Dweck, S. (2006) *Mindset: The New Psychology of Success*. New York: Random House.

Engle, R.W. (2002) Working memory capacity as executive attention, *Current Directions in Psychological Science*, 11(1): 19–23.

Fry, H. (2015) *The Mathematics of Love*. London: Simon & Schuster.

Fuson, K. (1988) *Children's Counting and Concept of Number*. New York: Springer.

Geary, D. and Hoard, M. (2005) Learning disabilities in arithmetic and mathematics: theoretical and empirical perspectives, in J.I.D. Campbell (ed.) *Handbook of Mathematical Cognition* (pp. 253–67). New York: Psychology Press.

Gelman, R. and Gallistel, C. (1986) *The Child's Understanding of Number*. Cambridge, MA: Harvard University Press.

Greenwood, J. (1984) My anxieties about math anxiety, *Mathematics Teacher*, 77: 662–3.

Gross, J., Hudson, C. and Price, D. (2009) *The Long Term Costs of Numeracy Difficulties*. London: Every Child a Chance Trust/ KPMG.

Joffe, L. (1980) Dyslexia and attainment in school mathematics: Part 2, *Dyslexia Review*, 3(2): 12–18.

Koshy, V., Ernert, P. and Casey, R. (1999) *Mathematics for Primary Teachers*. London: Routledge.

Mercer, N. and Sams, C. (2006) Teaching children how to use language to solve maths problems, *Language and Education*, 20(6): 507–28.

Parsons, S. and Bynner, J. (2005) *Does Numeracy Matter More?* London: National Research and Development Centre for Adult Literacy and Numeracy, Institute of Education.

Piazza, M., Fumarola, A., Chinello, A. and Melcher, D. (2011) Subitizing reflects visuo-spatial object individuation capacity, *Cognition*, 121(1): 147–53.

Price, G., Holloway, I., Räsänen, P., Vesterinen, M. and Ansari, D. (2007) Impaired parietal magnitude processing in developmental dyscalculia, *Current Biology*, 17(24): R1042–3.

Rawson, M. (1984) The Margaret Byrd Rawson Institute [retrieved from: http://mbri.org/; accessed 25 September 2016].

Schifter, D. (2007) What's right about looking at what's wrong?, *Making Math Count*, 65(3): 22–7.

Schwartz, L. (2001) *A Mathematician Grappling with His Century*. Basel: Birkhauser.

Sharma, M. (1987) How to take a child from concrete to abstract, *The Math Notebook*, 5: 8–10.

Starkey, P. and Cooper, R. (1980) Perception of numbers by human infants, *Science*, 210(4473): 1033–5.

Vygotsky, L.S. (1978) *Mind in Society: The development of higher psychological processes.* Cambridge, MA: Harvard University Press.

Williams, P. (2008) *The Independent Review of Mathematics Teaching in Early Years Settings and Primary Schools: Final report.* London: DCSF [retrieved from: http://childrens-mathematics.net/williams_maths_review.pdf].

Maths anxiety

A teacher must do more than just prepare great lessons. Success for many children is related to how we make them feel in class.

Fiore (1999: 403)

Before looking at what dyscalculia is in detail, we need to examine how maths anxiety impedes mathematical development. Dyscalculia and maths anxiety tend to go hand in hand. For many children the real root of their difficulties can be maths anxiety rather than a fundamental difficulty with maths. This maths anxiety can be intrinsically linked to negative experiences both at home and at school. It can be unwittingly transmitted from parents and teachers. Somewhat surprisingly, this transmission of anxiety from parent to child can be related to how much homework the parents do with their child (Maloney et al. 2015). This study looked to explore how parental anxiety about maths related to their children's achievement in maths. The researchers found that,

> ... when parents are more maths anxious, their children learn significantly less maths over the school year and have more maths anxiety by the school year's end, but only if maths anxious parents report providing frequent help with maths homework. Notably, when parents reported helping with maths homework less often, children's maths achievement and attitudes were not related to parents' maths anxiety.

(Maloney et al. 2015: 1480)

So, a maths anxious parent may think they are helping, but they are actually conveying their own anxiety and attitudes to maths whenever they sit down to do some maths with their son or daughter.

Teachers can also perpetuate this maths anxiety, if they themselves are not very confident. By avoiding questions and discussions about maths, they help to reinforce the idea that maths is difficult, stressful, and somewhat mysterious. Furthermore, we know that working memory, which we use in mental calculations, is very susceptible to anxiety (Ashcraft and Kirk 2001). When a dyscalculic child attempts a mathematical task, it is doubly hard for them as they are effectively trying to do two things at once. They not only have to do the maths but they also have to try to suppress their anxiety in order to be able to do the maths.

Mathematical shutdown/pseudo-dyscalculia

When we are in a stressful situation, our bodies produce adrenalin to fuel our natural 'fight or flight' reaction. In the classroom, we do not have the option of fight or flight, so our bodies produce more adrenalin, trying to make us react. Over time, some children will develop a Pavlovian response to this stress. The body learns that maths causes stress, and that it is not responding in a helpful way to the adrenalin, so goes straight to 'shut down'. In effect, the child programs herself to mentally shut down whenever faced with maths. The effect of this can be so severe that it appears that the child cannot do any maths at all, but really it is the anxiety that is the barrier, not the maths. This condition is sometimes referred to as *pseudo-dyscalculia*. A child who has this level of anxiety around maths will find it very hard to learn any maths until they have been taught how to overcome their fear and anxiety. This is a very significant problem that affects around a quarter of the population, and this chapter explores how to identify maths anxiety and how best to help learners with this condition.

Although maths anxiety was first recognized in the 1950s, we still have a limited understanding of it. However, there has been recent research on the effects of maths anxiety. Young et al. (2012), in a functional MRI study of 7- to 9-year-olds, found that there was increased activity in the area of the brain associated with negative emotions in the children with maths anxiety and that these levels of anxiety were specific to maths and unrelated to general anxiety, intelligence, working memory or reading ability. Furthermore, the maths anxiety experienced by these children was found to compromise the activity in the problem-solving areas of the brain, making it much harder for them to carry out mathematical tasks.

Identifying maths anxiety

There are many definitions of maths anxiety. What they all have in common is a focus around the level of anxiety affecting the individual's ability to carry out mathematical calculations both academically and in daily life.

Learners may present with both physical and psychological symptoms. The physical symptoms may include:

● Nail and lip biting
● Stomach aches
● Clammy hands
● Tension headaches
● Clenched fists
● Increase in heartbeat
● Being short of breath
● Dry mouth.

Any psychological symptoms could include:

● Low self-esteem
● Extreme nervousness and anxiety
● Confusion and disorganized thought
● Inability to retain or recall information.

These symptoms may be more noticeable when a learner is under time pressure or when 'put on the spot' to answer a question in front of their peers.

There are a few assessments that can be used to measure maths anxiety. Hunt et al. (2011) have developed the Maths Anxiety Scale-UK (MAS-UK) for adolescents and adults. It consists of 23 items that assess three different areas of anxiety:

● anxiety about being watched or evaluated while doing maths;
● anxiety of doing everyday maths, such as splitting a bill in a restaurant;
● anxiety watching someone else do maths.

The questions are designed to assess anxiety in each of these three areas. For example:

- calculating how many days until a friend's birthday;
- watching a teacher writing calculations on the board;
- adding up a pile of loose change;
- having someone watch you while you multiply 12 × 23 on a piece of paper.

These same researchers have also developed a Numeracy Apprehension Rating Scale for children in the Foundation Stage and Key Stage 1 (Petronzi 2016). This assessment consists of 19 items. The children rate their anxiety using three emoticons: happy, indifferent, and sad:

Their research has shown that even very young children can be apprehensive about maths. These children were seeing numeracy as being competitive and hierarchical. They were also linking fear and failure and were conscious of being 'punished' in some way if they did not achieve in maths, for example, being kept in at playtime.

Reducing maths anxiety

Reys et al. (2007) described maths anxiety as the gorge separating the 'concrete from the abstract'. Learners with maths difficulties need plenty of time and a non-threatening environment to cross this gorge. They also need the appropriate equipment to help them to get across. Without this support, they are likely to fall into the anxiety gorge and it will be very hard for them to climb out.

Strategies to reduce maths anxiety

Use concrete materials

If a learner can physically 'see' the maths and has apparatus that they can use to model the maths, then they will have a much better chance of understanding what they are doing. A great deal of anxiety is caused by maths being too abstract too soon. Materials such as

Cuisenaire rods, Numicon or base ten (Dienes) materials, counters and cubes can all help with understanding mathematical concepts.

Generate pictorial representations

Representing the concepts pictorially, for example through diagrams, drawings, and models, will help to bridge the gap between the concrete and the abstract. Many learners find this very hard to do but it is worth the effort, as it helps the learner to visualize the maths and to retain an image of the mathematical concept.

Look for connections and patterns

Maths becomes much easier if you can spot the patterns and connections. For example, if you know that $3 + 4 = 7$, then you will also be able to calculate $30 + 40$ and $300 + 400$ if you can see the pattern. For learners with specific difficulties in maths, this is not an easy task, so these patterns and connections need to be explicitly demonstrated.

Focus on understanding rather than memorizing

A learner's difficulty with maths often stems from memory issues, so they are unlikely to be able to remember procedures and number facts easily. If the learning has not been underpinned with understanding, the learner will have 'nowhere to go' if they forget something. However, if the focus has been on understanding rather than rote recall, they will more likely be able to remember or reconstruct the fact or procedure.

Create a safe environment

Most of us will be able to recall a stressful time in our own maths education. I remember times tables tests where the whole class had to stand up and answer quick fire times table questions. If you got the answer right you could sit down, but if you were wrong you had to remain standing. Imagine the stress and anxiety of being the last one standing, with all your peers watching you. Classroom scenarios like this contribute enormously to maths anxiety. Happily, classrooms today are generally less threatening, but it is still really important to make sure that the learning environment is as non-threatening as possible. Redefining our attitude to mistakes is also very valuable. We need to foster the attitude that mistakes are good and all part of the learning process in maths. Mistakes should be seen as a learning opportunity. One of the techniques used by teachers to promote a growth mindset is to select 'my favourite mistake'. The idea is for the teacher to review all the mistakes made by the class and select the one that they think will help the class to learn the most from. Exploring and analysing mistakes like this can provide insight into what has and has not been understood, and will also help those who are a little unsure to clarify their thinking and reasoning.

Encourage questions and answer them fully

Questioning in maths should always be a two-way process, with the learner being encouraged to ask as many questions as the teachers do. The sorts of questions that the learner asks will help you to assess the level of their understanding of a particular concept. Posing questions will also help them to develop their use of mathematical language. If answered sensitively and fully, then it will also help to reduce maths anxiety as the learners will be safe in the knowledge that there are no 'stupid' questions and that anything they do ask will be answered in full.

Show that you enjoy maths

Learners who have specific difficulties with maths will not enjoy it. None of us like to spend time doing things that we find hard and that make us feel bad. So time spent conveying a positive image of maths is time well spent and will hopefully help these learners to see that maths can be enjoyable and that it is achievable, albeit challenging at times. At the end of this book there is a section on some of the curiosities in maths and some of the activities that I pursue with learners, just for fun. They are not part of the National Curriculum and no-one will ever be tested on them, they are just there for the sheer beauty and enjoyment of maths. I thoroughly recommend them to you.

Avoid putting children into ability sets

Maths is a very diverse subject and just because a learner has difficulty in one area, it does not mean that they will experience difficulty in all areas. Putting children into sets will help predetermine their potential and will effectively cap their attainment, furthering their belief that they are bad at maths. Children are very aware of what set they are in, however cunningly we try and disguise it. My children were set in Reception and they all knew that it was better to be a tiger than a frog!

By placing children in mixed ability groups, we expose the ones who may be struggling to new ideas and different ways of thinking, something that they would probably not be exposed to if they were grouped by ability. Furthermore, the more able children will have the opportunity to support the children who are finding the work challenging.

Value and encourage persistence and resilience

All of us will find maths difficult at times. The key to this is how we react. Do we give up at the first sign of trouble or do we persevere? One message that we can convey to the learner who is finding it difficult is that it is okay to find it difficult. Hannah Fry (2016) put this very well when she described this as 'feeling comfortable with being uncomfortable'. In other words, learners need to believe that it is perfectly normal to find some aspects of maths challenging. In fact, if it is never challenging they won't be making the progress that they should be making.

Encourage the use of intuition

This is a tricky one because learners who are struggling with maths may not have much intuition, or 'gut feeling' for what is right, and even if they do, they may not have much faith in it. However, mathematicians use intuition, conjecture, and guesswork all the time. It is worth trying to develop this as much as possible.

Other techniques to reduce maths anxiety

Another strategy that has been found to help is to practise relaxation techniques. The individual will find it very hard to learn anything when they are in a state of anxiety, so teaching them how to relax will help them prepare for their learning.

1   *Deep breathing.* Sheffield and Hunt (2007) have found that relaxation techniques such as deep breathing can help to reduce

maths anxiety. This is a very simple and effective way to relax, as it naturally slows down the body's response to stress. Even very young children can be taught how to use this technique.

- Breathe in deeply.
- Hold the breath for a moment or two.
- Slowly release.
- Repeat as many times as necessary.

A variation on this is to try to slow down your breathing, to a rate of about ten breaths per minute. You can model this for the children so that they can practise breathing at this rate alongside you.

2   *Stretching.* Stretching can help to release tension in the muscles. One way to do this is to isolate different muscle groups and then stretch and relax them in turn.

3   *Exercise.* Exercise can really help children to relax, particularly if they are exercising to music. Timetabling maths lessons to follow break time or PE lessons could be a useful option.

4   *Visualization.* This is a surprisingly effective technique that is easy to achieve. The learner will need to imagine a place, feeling or event that is safe, relaxing or enjoyable just before they do a maths test or other stressful maths activity (Shobe et al. 2005). The effect is further enhanced if the learner practises deep breathing and muscle relaxation before the visualization. Soothing sounds or smells can also be used to good effect.

5   *Writing down your anxieties.* Recording your worries around maths can be quite cathartic and can help you to 'let go' of any anxieties, particularly if you do this prior to a stressful maths situation such as a test or exam. Writing for 10–15 minutes before a test means that the brain concentrates on writing rather than worrying (Ramirez and Beilock 2011).

6   *Music.* Playing soothing music as a background to maths lessons can also help to create a calm, relaxing environment.

7   *Laughter.* Ford et al. (2012) found that learners' anxiety was reduced if they had been shown a humorous cartoon prior to a stressful maths activity. Laughter is a good way of relieving tension, so having a bank of funny cartoons and maths jokes can be a useful and light-hearted strategy. There are many playground maths jokes. Here are just a couple:

'What did number 0 say to number 8?'
'Nice belt!'

'Why was 6 scared of 7?'
'Because 7 8 9!'

For many children, their anxiety around maths is the real barrier to their learning and unless we can overcome said barrier it will be very difficult for them to make any significant progress in maths.

References

Ashcraft, M. and Kirk, E. (2001) The relationships among working memory, math anxiety, and performance, *Journal of Experimental Psychology: General*, 130: 224–37.

Fiore, G. (1999) Math abused children: are we prepared to teach them?, *The Mathematics Teacher*, 92(5): 403–6.

Ford, T., Ford, B., Boxer, C. and Armstrong, J. (2012) Effect of humour on state anxiety and maths performance, *Humour*, 25(1): 59–74.

Fry, H. (2016) *Maths No Problem! The Confident Maths Teacher Conference Q&A, with Dr Hannah Fry*, London [retrieved from: https://www.youtube.com/watch?v=Fxp9RwygPFQ; accessed 25 September 2016].

Hunt, T.E., Clark-Carter, D. and Sheffield, D. (2011) The development and part validation of a UK scale for mathematics anxiety, *Journal of Psychoeducational Assessment*, 29(5): 455–66.

Maloney, E., Ramirez, G., Gunderson, E., Levine, S. and Beilock, S. (2015) Intergenerational effects of parents' maths anxiety on children's math achievement and anxiety, *Psychological Science*, 26(9): 1480–8.

Petronzi, D. (2016) The development of the Numeracy Apprehension Scale for children aged 4–7 years: qualitative exploration of associated factors and quantitative testing, PhD thesis, University of Derby [http://derby.openrepository.com/derby/handle/10545/619167].

Ramirez, G. and Beilock, S.L. (2011) Writing about testing worries boosts exam performance in the classroom, *Science*, 331: 211–13.

Reys, R., Lindquist, M., Lambdin, D. and Smith, N. (2007) *Helping Children Learn Mathematics*. Hoboken, NJ: Wiley.

Sheffield, D. and Hunt, T. (2007) How does anxiety influence maths performance and what can we do about it?, *MSOR Connections*, 6(4): 19–23.

Shobe, E., Brewin, A. and Carmack, S. (2005) A simple visualization exercise for reducing test anxiety and improving performance on difficult math tests, *Journal of Worry and Affective Experience*, 1(1): 34–52.

Young, C., Wu, S. and Menon, V. (2012) The neurodevelopmental basis of math anxiety, *Psychological Science*, 23(5): 492–501.

CHAPTER

3

Memory

My brain is like the Bermuda Triangle. Information goes in and is never seen again.

Anon

Memory and maths

Many learners' problems with maths stem from difficulties that they have with memory, whether it be short-term, long-term or working memory issues. This chapter is devoted to memory because it is such a complex subject and is so fundamental to our mathematical development.

Memory is an umbrella term that is used to describe the complex system of encoding, storing, and retrieving information. This information can be received through any of the five senses. Figure 3.1 shows how we deal with the information that bombards our senses all of the time. We filter much of it out and then decide what we actually need to attend to. This then feeds into our short-term memory, where we again filter out what we don't need to remember and transfer what we do need to remember to our long-term memory, which is akin to a filing cabinet storage system in the brain. In this very basic model, based on that of Atkinson and Shiffrin (1968), we can divide memory into a series of stores and view memory as information flow between these stores.

Sensory memory has a duration of between $\frac{1}{4}$ and $\frac{1}{2}$ of a second and has a very large capacity for all our sensory experience. There are different stores in the sensory memory for each of the senses.

In contrast, *short-term memory* is available for up to 18 seconds and has a much more limited capacity, usually around seven items. We use it for storing information without manipulating it mentally, or doing something else at the same time. There are two types of

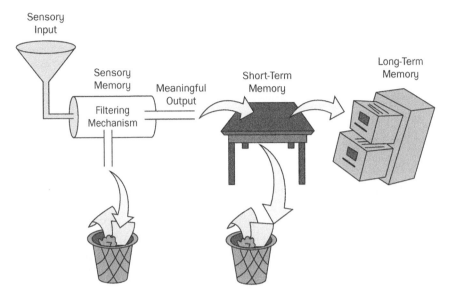

Figure 3.1 How we process information

short-term memory, verbal short-term memory and visuospatial short-term memory. Remembering a telephone number uses verbal short-term memory, as it is to do with recalling information that we have perceived aurally. Picking out a top to match the skirt you have just bought uses visuospatial memory, as it is to do with recalling information that has been perceived visually.

When information is no longer needed in short-term memory, it is discarded. Information in short-term memory is very fragile and is easily lost through distraction. However, if we want to use the information, then we need to store it in the short-term *working memory*. This allows us to hold on to the information while we work with it or manipulate it in some way, such as while we carry out a mental calculation (e.g. 23×25). In this instance, we may think of this as $(20 \times 25) + (3 \times 25)$. We would need to hold 20×25 in our working memory, while we calculate 3×25 and then add the two products together to give us the answer to 23×25 (i.e. 575).

The two areas of the short-term working memory system – visuospatial short-term memory and verbal short-term memory – are controlled by the *central executive* (Gathercole and Packiam Alloway 2008), as shown in Figure 3.2. The central executive controls information going to and coming from these distinct areas of short-term memory. It acts as a two-way system between the central executive and each of visuospatial and verbal short-term memory.

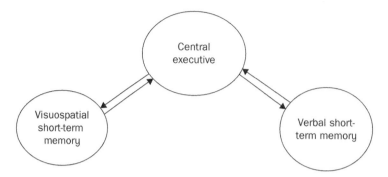

Figure 3.2 Model of working memory

If there are difficulties with processing information in visuospatial short-term memory, this can lead to faulty information being stored long term by the central executive. Examples of this faulty storage would be confusing the orientation of similar letters, such as b/d and p/q or confusing simlar symbols, such as 'X' and '+'. There may also be confusion over similar words, such as 'chip' and 'clip' or tranposing errors, such as writing 37 for 73. In contrast, if there are difficulties with processing information in verbal short-term memory, this can lead to faulty representations of the sounds in words, or the sequence of the sounds in words. For example, mistaking 'ch' for 'sh' or 'f' for 'th' .

The Baddeley and Hitch model of working memory

Another model of working memory (Baddeley and Hitch 1974) refers to the two areas of short-term memory as the visuospatial sketch pad and the phonological loop (also known as the articulatory loop), as shown in Figure 3.3.

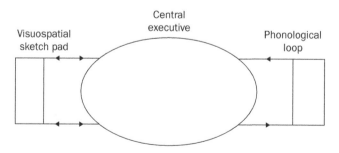

Figure 3.3 The articulatory loop

The phonological/articulatory loop

The phonological loop consists of two parts working in tandem. The first is the *phonological store*, which can be thought of as a tape recording loop that retains the most recent 2 seconds of auditory information that has been recorded. The second is the *articulatory control process*, which provides input to the phonological loop initially but also can refresh information already in the loop so that it can be stored for longer than 2 seconds.

Phonological memory refers to how we code information phonologically in working memory for temporary storage in short-term memory. When you attempt to remember a phone number you have looked up, as you make your way to the phone, you are storing the number temporarily in working memory. You probably do so not by storing a visual representation of the sequence of digits (although you may be able to do this if you try), but rather by storing a phonological representation of the sounds of the digit names. We often do this by repeating the number over and over again, until we have either made the call or found some paper to write it down on.

So, the phonological loop provides a brief, verbatim storage of auditory information (Baddeley 1986; Torgesen 1996). It is used for remembering serial information, such as phone numbers or multi-step instructions. It is very important in language learning, as it preserves the order in which words are presented and acts as a temporary storage for unfamiliar words, while prior knowledge is accessed that will help us to understand these new words.

The efficiency of the phonological loop can be measured using a number of tests, including the digit span test, rapid naming test, and semantic fluency test.

Digit span test

One of the simplest tests to undertake is a digit span test (Turner and Ridsdale 2004). In this test, the administrator reads out a sequence of digits, one second apart in a monotone voice. The participant then repeats back the sequence of digits in the order in which they were presented. This sequence starts with just a couple of numbers before increasing to three, four, etc. until the participant fails to recall the sequence correctly on a set number of occasions (usually twice). Typically, we will be able to recall around 7 or 8 digits presented in this way. This is the first part of the test and assesses verbal short-term memory (see Table 3.1a). The test is now repeated with a different set of sequences, but this time the participant has to repeat the sequence in reverse order (see Table 3.1b). So if 3 . . . 6 . . . 2 was presented, the participant would have to respond 2 . . . 6 . . . 3. This repeating in reverse order is an assessment of working memory, as we have to recall the sequence and then manipulate it, by reversing it. Typically, performance on reverse recall is two items fewer than on straight repetition. In other words, if you can repeat 7 digits forwards, you would be expected to be able to repeat 5 digits in reverse order. A more marked discrepancy would be a good indication that the participant has working memory difficulties.

Table 3.1 Digit span test

(a) Digits forwards

Item	Trial 1	√ or ×	Trial 2	√ or ×	Total
A	43		16		
B	792		847		
C	5941		7253		
D	93872		75396		
E	152649		216748		
F	3745261		4925316		
G	82973546		69174253		
H	246937185		371625948		
				Forwards score:	

(b) Digits backwards

Item	Trial 1	√ or ×	Trial 2	√ or ?	Total
A	83		29		
B	475		615		
C	2619		3852		
D	28736		59413		
E	624719		276391		
F	4183627		1586937		
G	52624197		94617385		
				Backwards score:	

Note: A full copy of this test can be found at: www.dyslexia-international.org/content/Informal%20 tests/Digitspan.pdf.

Rapid naming test

A second test that can be used is the rapid naming test, which measures the functioning of the central executive. In this test, participants are presented with a sequence of letters, digits, colours or objects (depending upon their age and the focus of the test) and their task is to correctly name the items in the right order as quickly as they can. This can be a measure of phonological awareness when letters are used, but is also a measure of the functioning of the central executive and can provide information on how quickly a person can process information. For many learners with maths difficulties, it can be the speed at which they process information that is the barrier to their learning.

There are many versions of the rapid naming test. Commonly used tests include the Comprehensive Test of Phonological Processing (Wagner et al. 2013) and the Phonological Assessment Battery (Gibbs and Bodman 2014).

Semantic fluency test

This is a very simple test, but one that can give you a fascinating insight into how information is being stored in the memory system. This test is one of the subtests of the Phonological Assessment Battery. For this test, the participant has 30 seconds to name as many items in a certain category as they can. For example, you could ask them to name as many foods as they can or items in their classroom. Some learners are incredibly systematic in their approach to this and may respond something like this:

> Apples, oranges, bananas, pears, peaches, chicken, beef, ham, pork, lamb, sausages, carrots, peas, potatoes, cabbage, etc.

It is clear that the information here has been categorized and stored in groups of related items. These learners can quickly access their store of information on fruit, meat, and vegetables and will therefore be able to quickly rattle off many items of food in 30 seconds. Other children will give you a random list of unrelated foods, for which there is no rhyme or reason, often with gaps in between while they search around in their memory for a relevant piece of information. This tells us a great deal about how information is being stored in the memory system and how well the learner can categorize. Being able to spot similarities and differences in maths can be very useful in helping us to generalize, to spot patterns, and to make connections. By administering this type of semantic fluency test, we can begin to understand the mechanics of the learner's memory system and how this may be impeding their progress in maths.

Generally speaking, learners with dyslexia will have difficulties with the functioning of the phonological loop. If the phonological loop is compromised in some way, then the central executive has to work harder in order to compensate and this will impact on the working memory in terms of how much information can be held in working memory or in terms of how long it can be stored for. This can explain why many dyslexic learners take more time to complete a task and also why they tire so easily, as their brains have to work much harder.

Visuospatial sketch pad

The visuospatial sketch pad is another name for visuospatial short-term memory. It is a parallel system to the phonological loop and is akin to an artist's sketchbook for stimuli that cannot be verbalized, such as spatial information. The visuospatial sketch pad deals with the storage and manipulation of information that is to do with colour, shape, and form. Generally speaking, learners with dyslexia don't have a problem with the visuospatial sketch pad. It is learners that have dyscalculia or dyspraxia that have difficulty with this area of the working memory system. Once we have understood this model of working memory, we can then begin to explain some of the specific difficulties that these learners have.

Dyslexia and the phonological loop

The working memory is a bi-directional system, so if there is a deficit in the function of the phonological loop, there will be a breakdown between it and the central executive. The central executive will become overburdened, which will have a negative impact on working memory. However, there tends to be no problem with the visuospatial sketch pad, which works well with the central executive. This explains why many dyslexic learners have good visuospatial awareness. They are often described as being able to see the 'Big Picture'.

They tend to take a holistic overview of problems rather than an analytical sequential approach.

Dyspraxia, dyscalculia, and the visuospatial sketch pad

Similarly, if there is a deficit in the function of the visuospatial sketch pad, this will also impact on the central executive function and consequently working memory. This can explain why many learners with dyspraxia or dyscalculia have difficulty with spatial awareness leading to problems interpreting two- and three-dimensional images and reading graphs.

Working memory

The working memory is central to the learning process and we rely on it in almost every aspect of our learning. Most children who have difficulty with academic achievement will have some sort of compromised function of the working memory.

Purposes of the working memory

We can examine the role of the working memory by looking at five distinct ways in which we use it when we are learning.

1   Holding an idea in mind while developing, elaborating, clarifying or using it. This is a function of the working memory that we need in order to work on and improve ideas and understanding. We may be making connections with prior knowledge or coming up with new ideas, but all the time we have to juggle lots of different pieces of information in our working memory.

2   Recalling information from long-term memory while holding related information in short-term memory. When we are trying to understand some new piece of information, we try and link it to something that we already know. This makes it much easier for us to process and retain the new information. In order to do this, we need to be able to access information from our long-term memory and then match it up with the new information that is being temporarily stored in our working memory.

3   Holding the components of a task together in memory while completing the task. This is particularly true when we are doing

maths, because we often have to hold part of a calculation in our working memory while we work on others parts, and then bring all the pieces back together to come up with our answer.

4   Keeping a series of pieces of information together so that they remain meaningful. When we are listening to, or reading, a long sentence we need to be able to keep track of what was being said at the beginning of the sentence to make sure that we can retain our comprehension.

5   Holding a long-term plan while thinking about a short-term need. This can also be described as starting with the end in mind. When we are writing a story, or planning an essay, we need to keep on track and have the end in mind throughout the writing process, so that we don't go off on a tangent. This is equally true in multistep calculations in maths, where we need to keep track of what we are trying to calculate, even though there may be many smaller steps on the way to the answer.

Indicators of working memory difficulties

Learners with working memory issues can display a wide range of behaviours. Some will appear to be very inattentive, as if they are not listening to a word that you are saying. This is particularly true if they have been given multiple instructions. They may well just stare back at you with a blank expression. This isn't because they have not been listening, it is because their working memory has been completely overloaded and has effectively collapsed. Other learners can be very easily distracted, impulsive or display 'immediate forget-fulness'. They can't keep information in their working memory for very long so will just flit from one thing to the next as information comes into, and almost immediately leaves, their working memory. Some learners will be very fidgety, always moving in an attempt to stay alert, and this can lead to tiredness and irritability.

All of these difficulties will lead to the learner being very frustrated and anxious about their learning and often will have a detrimental effect on their self-esteem. The difficulties that learners have with working memory can be located in either the phonological loop or the visuospatial sketch pad, or both, and can be defined in terms of capacity and time.

Capacity refers to how much information can be stored in the working memory at any one time. This is sometimes referred to as the *neurological scratch pad*. Most people can retain up to seven separate items in their working memory, but for people with poor working memory capacity this can be as few as three items.

Time refers to how long the information can be stored. If individual pieces of information are presented too far apart, it can be very hard to retain that information completely and in the correct sequence.

Long-term memory

In addition to this working memory system, there is also an area devoted to long-term memory. We can choose to select information from the working memory to store in long-term memory. The long-term memory is a system for permanently storing, managing, and retrieving information for later and ongoing use. Items of information stored as long-term memories can be accessible for the whole of our lives.

Components of long-term memory

Long-term memories can be explicit or implicit. *Explicit memory* refers to information that we consciously bring to mind, for example, Paris being the capital of France. *Implicit memory*, on the other hand, refers to information that we don't need to consciously bring to mind, for example, how to ride a bike or how to skip. Figure 3.4 shows the different areas of our memory system. We can see that implicit memory relates to procedures, such as skills and tasks that we carry out on a daily basis without any conscious thought. Explicit memory can also be referred to as declarative memory and this in turn can be split into episodic and semantic memory. Episodic memoy relates to events and experiences, such as our wedding day. Semantic memory relates to facts and concepts, such as knowing that $3 \times 5 = 15$ and that multiplication and division are inverse operations.

Any impairment of the sensory organs will prevent information from being clearly registered in the memory system. Difficulties can also occur with the transfer of information from short-term to long-term memory and also in retrieval of information from memory. As we have seen, short-term and working memory have a limited capacity, in terms of the number of items that can be stored, much like a shelf. If you put too many items on the shelf, something will either fall off or the shelf will collapse completely, a phenomenon referred

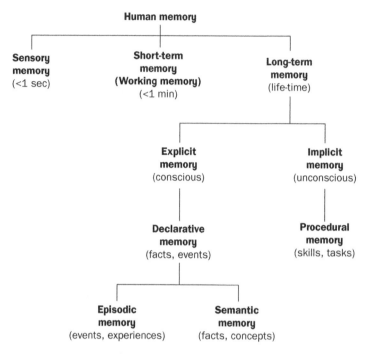

Figure 3.4 The different areas of the memory system

to as catastrophic memory loss. Short-term and working memory also have a limited capacity in terms of how long we can hold the information for. This can vary from just a few seconds to several minutes. Most learners who have academic difficulties will have poor working memory capacity.

Working memory difficulties can affect:

● how well someone can plan or sequence activities;
● how well they can attend to information;
● how well they can cope with distraction;
● how they use feedback and learn from mistakes;
● how well they can cope with change or new information.

The implications are that we need to make sure that we assess working memory when we are trying to identify the cause of maths difficulties. Many learners are presenting with dyscalculic-type difficulties when in fact it is a deficit in working memory that is the problem (Mammarella et al. 2015).

References

Atkinson, R. and Shiffrin, R. (1968) Human memory: a proposed system and its control processes, in K. Spence and J. Spence (eds) *The Psychology of Learning and Motivation*, Vol. 2 (pp. 89–195). New York: Academic Press.

Baddeley, A. (1986) *Working Memory*. Oxford: Oxford University Press.

Baddeley, A. and Hitch, G. (1974) Working memory, in G.H. Bower (ed.) *The Psychology of Learning and Motivation: Advances in research and theory*, Vol. 8 (pp. 47–89). New York: Academic Press.

Gathercole, S. and Packiam Alloway, T. (2008) *Working Memory and Learning*. London: Sage.

Gibbs, S. and Bodman, S. (2014) *Phonological Assessment Battery* (2nd edn.). Swindon: GL Assessment.

Mammarella, I., Hill, F., Devine, A., Caviola, S. and Szűcs, D. (2015) Math anxiety and developmental dyscalculia: a study on working memory processes, *Journal of Clinical and Experimental Neuropsychology*, 37(8): 878–87.

Torgesen, J. (1996) A model of memory from an informational processing perspective: the special case of phonological memory, in G.R. Lyon and N.A. Krasnegor (eds) *Attention, Memory and Executive Function* (pp. 157–84). Baltimore, MD: Brookes.

Turner, M. and Ridsdale, J. (2004) *The Digit Memory Test*. York: University of York.

Wagner, R., Torgesen, J., Rashotte, C. and Pearson, N. (2013) *CTOPP-2: Comprehensive Test of Phonological Processing* (2nd edn.). Austin, TX: PRO-ED Inc.

Dyscalculia

The greatest unsolved theorem in mathematics is why some people are better at Maths than others.

Adrian Mathesis (cited in Eves 1987; see www.math.pitt.edu/~wjl/MathQuotes.html)

What is dyscalculia?

Dyscalculia is generally thought of as a specific learning difficulty in mathematics, or, more particularly, arithmetic. The word 'dyscalculia' has both Greek and Latin roots and literally means 'counting badly': the Greek prefix 'dys', which means badly and the Latin 'calculare', which means 'to count'. Dyscalculia is a condition that is still yet to be categorically defined. Several organizations and individual researchers have proposed their own definitions and this chapter will explore common threads and also examine the implications of the differences between the various definitions.

Kosc was one of the first people to attempt to define dyscalculia and he described developmental dyscalculia as

> . . . a structural disorder of mathematical abilities which has its origin in a genetic or congenital disorder in those parts of the brain that are the anatomical-physiological substrate of the maturation of the mathematical abilities adequate to age, without a simultaneous disorder of general mental functions.
>
> (Kosc 1974: 165)

Kosc has highlighted the specificity of dyscalculia, in that a person's difficulties are specific to the field of mathematics and are not general in nature, and also that the difficulties are located in the parts of the brain that are responsible for mathematical cognitive function. In practice, this definition refers to children who present as capable in all academic areas other than maths.

The *Diagnostic and Statistical Manual of Mental Disorders IV* (DSM-IV), used widely by educational psychologists, refers to dyscalculia as a mathematics disorder in terms of test scores

> . . . as measured by a standardized test that is given individually, the person's mathematical ability is substantially less than would be expected from the person's age, intelligence and education. This deficiency materially impedes academic achievement or daily living.
>
> (APA 2000: 315.1)

The DSM-IV definition does not specifically use the term dyscalculia, but it is similar to Kosc's definition in that it describes the disorder as unexpected. This is a key factor in identifying learners with dyscalculia. Generally, people with dyscalculia function perfectly well in all other areas, yet they have a specific and unexplained difficulty with maths.

The DSM-IV also goes on to state that 'This deficiency materially impedes academic achievement or daily living' (APA 2000: 315.1). This is an important point to make, as the impact on daily life should not be underestimated. We rely on maths for so many of our daily activities, yet dyscalculic adults often have difficulty with many day-to-day activities such as managing their finances and finding the best value items when shopping. They can often be isolated because they find it difficult to understand the scoring systems of games and sports. They may also never learn to drive because of the intrinsic numerical demands that driving entails. Time management can also be problematic. Many dyscalculic adults have trouble using public transport since they are unable to extract the relevant information from timetables or they have difficulty planning the time required for journeys and thus often miss their train or bus.

The DSM-IV definition has now been superseded by the DSM-V (APA 2013: 315.1), which does not refer to dyscalculia specifically, but does refer to a *specific learning disorder* with impairment in maths, under the more general heading of 'neurodevelopmental disorders'. These are defined as 'Disorders with onset in the developmental period, often before starting school, and are characterized by a range of developmental deficits that impair normal functioning.' It defines specific learning disorder as:

> A neurodevelopmental disorder of biological origin manifested in learning difficulties and problems in acquiring academic skills markedly below age level and manifested in the early school years, lasting for at least six months; not attributed to intellectual disabilities, developmental disorders, or neuro-logical or motor disorders.
>
> (APA 2013: 315.1)

The DSM-V confirms dyscalculia, termed maths impairment, as a specific learning difficulty. The implications of this for educators is that they are bound by the Equality Act (2010) that reasonable adjustments are made to ensure that the needs of learners with dyscalculia are met in the classroom.

The National Numeracy Strategy offers the following definition:

> Dyscalculia is a condition that affects the ability to acquire arithmetical skills. Dyscalculic learners may have difficulty understanding simple number concepts, lack an intuitive grasp of numbers, and have problems learning number facts and pro-cedures. Even if they produce a correct answer or use a correct method, they may do so mechanically and without confidence.
>
> (DfES 2001: 2)

This definition has not been updated since 2001 and a search for 'dyscalculia' on the current DfES website offers zero results for dyscalculia compared with 49 for dyslexia. Despite this, the 2001 definition is useful because it refers to 'a lack of an intuitive grasp of number' and this is one of the key indicators of dyscalculia, often referred to as a lack of number sense.

The British Dyslexia Association (BDA) is now offering training for teachers in dyscalculia and they have adopted a more current definition from the American Psychiatric Association:

> Developmental Dyscalculia (DD) is a specific learning disorder that is characterised by impairments in learning basic arithmetic facts, processing numerical magnitude and performing accurate and fluent calculations. These difficulties must be quantifiably

below what is expected for an individual's chronological age, and must not be caused by poor educational or daily activities or by intellectual impairments.

(BDA 2017)

Again, there is reference to the unexpected and unexplained nature of dyscalculic difficulties and also mention of numerical magnitude processing. Professor Brian Butterworth, among others, has researched the ability of a person with dyscalculia to assess numerical magnitude and this forms part of his screening tool for dyscalculia.

The reference to being able to perform calculations fluently is also worthy of note. Fluency is now one of three key skills that have been highlighted in the new National Curriculum (DfE 2014), alongside problem-solving and mathematical reasoning. Many dyscalculic learners will learn the procedure and some may be able to apply it consistently but very few do so with any degree of fluency.

Dehaene (2011) describes dyscalculic children as those with normal perception, language, and intelligence, who exhibit disproportionate difficulties with number processing and arithmetic. Magnetic resonance imaging (MRI) scans suggest that there is less grey matter in the left intraparietal sulcus of these children, the area of the brain that is active during mental arithmetic tasks. Deheane also proposes the idea of number sense as something that is innate in humans but is missing in learners with dyscalculia. He attributes this to lesions on the brain that affect mathematical ability. This definition links well with that of Kosc in terms of trying to pinpoint dyscalculia to a specific area of the brain. Brian Butterworth (2005a) also believes that developmental dyscalculics have reduced grey matter in the left parietal lobe (Isaacs et al. 2001) and that this is the area responsible for numerical processing.

Price and Ansari (2013) concur with this view of dyscalculia. They attribute it to 'an underlying deficit in the representation and processing of numerical magnitude information.' An earlier definition comes from Sharma (1997), who defined dyscalculia as:

An inability to conceptualise numbers, number relationships (arithmetical facts) and the outcomes of numerical operations (estimating the answer to numerical problems before actually calculating).

This is a more operational definition, explaining the effects of dyscalculia and enabling practitioners and individuals to begin to ascertain whether the mathematics difficulties are general or of a more specific dyscalculic origin. It also refers us back to the idea of number sense, introduced by Dehaene and which is really at the heart of dyscalculia.

Domain-specific and domain-general definitions

The above definitions can be categorized into those which are domain-specific and those which are domain-general. *Domain-specific* definitions identify one core deficit, namely in the left parietal lobe, which is responsible for number processing. In contrast, domain-general definitions suggest a multiple deficit model, with different areas of the brain being implicated via their interplay with each other. Muter (2013) suggests that cognitive functioning appears to depend on how a specific brain region interacts with other regions in the brain.

Implications for teaching

The implications of these definitions to teaching practice are to consider whether a learner in your class:

- is experiencing persistent and extreme difficulty in mathematics;
- is generally able in all other areas of the curriculum;
- has difficulties in maths that are unexpected and unexplained by external factors.

The key issue here is the unexpected nature of the difficulty. People with dyscalculia often function very well in all other areas.

The differences in definitions reflect the different theoretical and research perspectives of different experts. Some experts define dyscalculia in terms of an underlying presumed genetic, constitutional or neuroanatomical immaturity in specific areas of the brain (Kosc 1974). Some definitions of dyscalculia are more general and do not presuppose any genetic or underlying neuroanatomical substrate. Having looked at several definitions, some common themes can be identified from which the basis for a working definition of dyscalculia can be formulated.

Working definition for dyscalculia

An unexplained, prolonged specific difficulty in mathematics, caused by structural differences in the areas of the brain responsible for numerical calculation.

Individuals with dyscalculia generally function well in all other areas, but display a complete lack of number sense and intuition for number. The effects of their difficulties in maths can be far-reaching and can significantly impair daily living.

Subtypes of dyscalculia

We can examine the definition of dyscalculia further by looking at the various subtypes that have been identified by researchers in this field. Price and Ansari (2013) refer to 'primary' and 'secondary' developmental dyscalculia:

- *Primary dyscalculia*: impaired development of brain mechanisms for processing numerical magnitude information.
- *Secondary dyscalculia*: mathematical deficits stemming from external factors such as poor teaching, low socio-economic status, and behavioural attention problems or domain-general cognitive deficits.

Kaufman et al. have proposed a new definition that also refers to primary and secondary dyscalculia:

Primary Developmental Dyscalculia is a heterogeneous disorder resulting from individual defects at behavioural, cognitive, neuro-psychological and neuronal levels. The term Secondary Developmental Dyscalculia should be used if numerical/arithmetic dysfunctions are caused by non-numerical impairments such as attention disorders.

(Kaufmann et al. 2013: 516)

Several researchers have suggested dividing dyscalculia into subtypes in an attempt to explore and explain the condition further. Karagiannakis and Cooreman (2015) have identified four subtypes of dyscalculia:

● Core number
● Reasoning
● Memory
● Visuospatial.

Examining these in detail can provide insight into the complexity and variability of dyscalculia. Some learners will have difficulty in all or maybe just one or two of these areas.

Core number

The first of the four subtypes of dyscalculia leads to difficulties with the following:

Basic number sense

Number sense is our ability to be flexible with number and to understand how numbers relate to each other. It can be seen as 'good intuition about numbers and their relationships. It develops gradually as a result of exploring numbers, visualizing them in a variety of contexts, and relating them in ways that are not limited by traditional algorithms' (Howden 1989: 11)

Learners with poor number sense rely on rote learning and applying procedures. The rarely use reasoning and generalizing as a means to tackling mathematical tasks. For example, a child with good number sense would see 29 + 30 + 31 as 3 × 30, as this is a quicker way of working out the answer. A child with poor number sense would not see the relationship between these numbers and would probably follow the standard procedure of column addition.

Estimating and rounding

Many learners with maths difficulties are reluctant to find an estimate before calculating an answer, but most will have some idea of the expected magnitude of the answer. Those with core number deficit will literally have no idea what the answer should be, so will accept any answer that they get, however implausible it may be.

Appreciating numerical quantity

As well as having difficulty in estimating, these learners will also find it hard to assess numerical quantity. Learners with dyscalculia have difficulty matching the numerical symbol to the numerical quantity. They also have difficulty comparing numerical quantities – for example, understanding that 370 is ten times as large as 37 and ten times smaller than 3700. In severe cases, they may find it hard to understand even basic comparisons, such as 8 being more than 6.

Working with mathematical symbols

The symbols that we use in maths are a form of arbitrary shorthand, to help us when we are recording mathematical ideas. Often, learners with core number difficulties find it very hard to understand and use mathematical symbols.

Place value

Place value is an abstract concept and one that many learners struggle with, for example, going through a stage of writing 1002 for 102 (one hundred and two). However, for learners with dyscalculia, place value can be a concept that they struggle with year on year.

Placing numbers on a number line

Another difficulty these learners have is placing numbers on a number line. This stems from the children not having an appreciation of how numbers relate to each other.

Reasoning

The second of the four subtypes of dyscalculia leads to difficulties with the following:

Understanding mathematical concepts and relationships

For many learners with difficulty in this area, maths is all about remembering procedures, times tables, and number bonds. They have very little understanding of the patterns and connections in maths, such as understanding the repeated addition and area models of multiplication or appreciating that we can use subtraction to check addition calculations.

Generalizing and transferring information

Being able to make connections in maths can make life much easier, as learners can use what they already know to work out something different. For example, if you know that $4 + 5 = 9$, then you can generalize this information to help work out $40 + 50$, $4 + 4$, etc. Learners with poor mathematical reasoning will not see these connections and will treat each calculation as completely new and discrete from anything they have met before.

Understanding multiple steps in complex procedures/algorithms

Learners with poor reasoning skills invariably have to rely on their memory when tackling maths problems. Some procedures in maths can be complex, involving multiple steps, and if you are relying solely on memory rather than understanding, it can be very easy to make mistakes and miss out steps.

Problem-solving and decision-making

Learners with poor reasoning skills find it hard to solve problems in different ways and tend to use the same method every time. This can be a very inefficient way of approaching maths problems and effectively means that they are doing a harder version of maths. For example, $2000 × 0.25$ is much easier to calculate if you think of 0.25 as being one-quarter and the you can just divide 2000 by 4.

Memory

The third of the four subtypes of dyscalculia leads to difficulties with the following:

Remembering and recalling numerical facts

This includes the recall of number bonds to ten or times tables. Without understanding how numbers relate to each other, all we can rely on is our memory to help us to remember these facts. For some learners, their short-term, working, and long-term memory can be compromised, leading to difficulties in maths – particularly in mental calculations.

Understanding and recalling mathematical terminology

Many words in maths are technical and not commonly used in daily language (e.g. numerator and denominator), which makes maths inaccessible for many learners. In contrast, other mathematical terms that are also in frequent daily use have multiple meanings, which can be a great cause of confusion. For example, words like 'table', 'product', and 'degree'.

Understanding word problems

As well as getting to grips with the mathematical language, learners also need to understand how it relates to real-life situations and be able to interpret the maths behind complex word problems. This requires the learner to be able to store verbal information in their working memory while accessing the maths that relates to that information. For learners with poor memory, this can be very challenging.

Performing mental calculations accurately

Mental arithmetic places great demands on working memory, with pieces of information having to be held while we work on something else and then correctly retrieved and integrated back into the original question. For example, think of all the separate pieces of information that you would need to hold in your head if you were to mentally calculate 43×25. You could split the 43 into 40 and 3 and multiply 40×25, then hold on to that fact while you multiply 3×25 before adding the two products together.

Keeping track of the steps in problem-solving

Again, this will place huge demands on working memory, as the learner will need to hold information in mind while following the steps of a procedure and also make sure that the steps are carried out in the correct order.

Visuospatial

The final of the four subtypes of dyscalculia leads to difficulties with the following:

Recognizing and understanding symbols

For example, many learners with dyscalculia confuse × with +. They can also have difficulty understanding commonly used symbols such as '='. Many learners think this sign means 'the answer is'. We often present equations in a way that perpetuates this misunderstanding, writing 2 + 3 = 5 rather than 5 = 2 + 3. This leads the learner to believe that '=' means 'the answer is' rather than 'equals'.

Interpreting visual representations of mathematical objects

Having poor visuospatial skills will make it hard to recognize the net of a square, or be able to visualize and describe a three-dimensional shape.

Placing numbers on a number line

A number line is a very versatile tool in maths but this versatility can be very confusing for the dyscalculic learner. A line of the same length could represent a range of one, ten, a million, anything in fact! Couple this with a lack of appreciation of how numbers relate to each other and it is easy to see how difficult placing numbers on a number line can be. For example, being able to place 60 in roughly the right place on a blank number line from 0 to 100 requires the learner to be able to visually split the line into relevant sections so that they can place the number in roughly the right place.

Interpreting graphs and tables

Dyscalculic learners with poor visuospatial skills have difficulty reading information from tables or understanding graphs and how to interpret them. They also have difficulty understanding scales on axes and measuring.

Further subtypes of developmental dyscalculia

In 2012, Tony Attwood identified five different types of dyscalculia, having submitted 300 children between the ages of 8 and 18 years to an online test to see if any patterns emerged.

- Type 1 dyscalculics have severe maths anxiety. Their difficulties in maths are largely attributed to this anxiety. These learners believe that they 'can't do maths' and this may have been exacerbated by a lack of appropriate support. They are only able to cope with the most basic calculations.
- Type 2 dyscalculics also have a level of maths anxiety but they have managed to find some compensatory strategies that help them to cope with basic maths. They have a functional understanding of maths, enough for them to deal with the mathematical demands of daily life. They tend to work slowly and are acutely aware of how 'slow' they are compared with others.
- Type 3 dyscalculics have profound difficulty comprehending and dealing with the concept of time. For these learners it is not just a question of not being able to tell the time – they literally have no concept of time. They have no idea whether five minutes or fifty minutes have passed. This can have a severe impact on daily living and may prevent them from holding down a job or having a social life. Type 3 dyscalculics may also have difficulty sequencing, particularly in describing a sequence of actions.
- The underlying problem of Type 4 dyscalculics is memory rather than a core number issue. These learners find it very hard to transfer information from the short-term to long-term memory, and find recalling times tables and mathematical procedures difficult. This type links well to the memory subtype identified by Karagiannakis and Cooreman (2015).
- Type 5 dyscalculics see maths as very abstract and find it hard to visualize mathematical concepts or to relate them to the real world. They struggle enormously with fractions and find it hard to relate fractions such as $\frac{1}{2}$ and a $\frac{1}{4}$ to real objects. For these children, $\frac{1}{2} + \frac{1}{4}$ may well be answered with $\frac{2}{6}$. This type also overlaps with the visuospatial subtype identified by Karagiannakis and Cooreman (2015).

Acalculia

There is one further type of dyscalculia that is worthy of mention – acalculia. Acalculia occurs as a result of a brain injury, such as after a stroke. In the brain, number symbols are processed and understood in the left parietal lobe. If this area is damaged, it can lead to a total lack of comprehension of numbers (Jackson and Warrington 1986). Acalculia can present in many forms. There have been cases where a person may still be able to do maths, but only if it is written in words rather than symbols, due to the damage to the number processing area of the brain.

So we can see that there are many viewpoints and many ways of categorizing dyscalculia and research is ongoing into how we define and understand this very complex learning difficulty.

Causes of dyscalculia

It is clear that dyscalculia can be a combination of genetic and environmental factors – in other words, internal and external factors. Researchers such as Price and Ansari (2013) have referred to these internal and external causes of dyscalculia as primary and secondary dyscalculia, respectively.

Internal causes: primary dyscalculia

Brain function

At the core of many definitions of dyscalculia lies a deficit in brain function. MRI scans have been used to identify areas in the brain that are thought to be responsible for dyscalculia. There appear to be differences in the surface area, thickness, and volume of parts of the brain that are used in memory and for keeping track of a task (Castelli et al. 2006).

The left parietal lobe, one of the four lobes in the brain, has been associated with maths difficulty since the beginning of the last century. Josef Gerstmann studied a group of patients who had lesions to the angular gyrus and who had difficulty with calculating, writing, distinguishing the fingers on their hands, and left/right confusion. This profile of symptoms is known as Gerstmann's syndrome.

Genetics

Studies have shown that a learner with dyscalculia often has a sibling or parent with similar mathematical difficulties. So it may be that dyscalculia is hereditary in the same way that dyslexia is (Shalev and Gross-Tsur 2001).

Prenatal influences

There is evidence linking dyscalculia with exposure to alcohol in the womb. Prematurity and low birthweight may also play a role in dyscalculia, as well as conditions such as Turner's syndrome (Murphy et al. 2006).

External causes: secondary dyscalculia

In Chapter 1 we explored some of the external causes that may lead children to have difficulty in maths, and it is important that these are ruled out when diagnosing dyscalculia.

Dyscalculia indicators

Thambirajah (2011) lists four signs of dyscalculia:

- difficulty understanding quantities and an inability to carry out age-appropriate arithmetic operations;
- the learner will be on the 5th percentile or lower for achievement;
- the learner's underachievement in maths will affect daily life; and
- the difficulties experienced will have been present since an early age and will not be due to external factors.

Skagerlund and Traff (2016) have suggested that children with dyscalculia display difficulties with space and time as well as number.

There is no single test for dyscalculia but there are several routes that we can take in order to reach a diagnosis. Teachers and/or parents will invariably have observed poor numeracy development in a child and this will prompt them to investigate the difficulty further. This is particularly true if the numerical difficulty is unexpected and unexplained.

An inability to subitize even very small quantities

The word 'subitize' comes from the Latin word 'subito', meaning 'suddenly'. It refers to our ability to immediately recognize the number of items in a set without actually having to count them. Most people can subitize up to six or seven items. A dyscalculic learner will not be able to do this and may have difficulty in subitizing just three items (Butterworth 2005b).

Most people will be able to instantly recognize that there are five dots in Figure 4.1 without having to count them. In contrast, almost all of us would need to count the dots in Figure 4.2, as there are so many of them. In contrast, a dyscalculic person might not be able to subitize even the two dots shown in Figure 4.3.

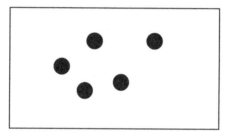

Figure 4.1 Subitizing five dots

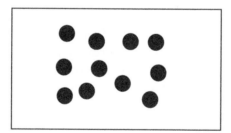

Figure 4.2 Counting dots

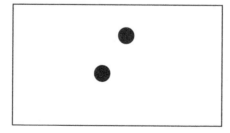

Figure 4.3 Subitizing two dots

The ability to subitize is something a person is born with. Klein and Starkey (1988) carried out an experiment to explore this ability. They showed a group of 72 babies aged 16 to 30 weeks old pictures of a number of dots and noted their fixation time for each picture. When shown two dots, their fixation time averaged 1.9 seconds, yet this rose to 2.5 seconds when shown three dots. This demonstrated that the babies could detect a change in numerical quantity. Brian Butterworth refers to this ability as 'numerosity'.

Being able to assess numerical quantity is in fact a survival instinct, so in a way it is not surprising that we are born with this innate sense of number. When our ancestors were hunting and gathering, they needed to be able to quickly assess numerical quantity. If one animal was coming towards you, this could be seen as an opportunity to bring home a decent meal. In contrast, if five animals were charging towards you, you would need to run away before you became the meal!

Poor number sense

Number sense refers to our ability to understand numbers and how they relate to each other. Someone with good number sense will know what they can and can't do with numbers and will be able to manipulate numbers and use them flexibly. Gersten and Chard (1999: 118) defined number sense as 'an emerging construct that refers to a child's fluidity and flexibility with numbers, the sense of what numbers mean and an ability to perform mental mathematics and to look at the world and make comparisons'. Number sense can be seen as a 'good intuition about numbers and their relationships. It develops gradually as a result of exploring numbers, visualizing them in a variety of contexts, and relating them in ways that are not limited by traditional algorithms' (Howden 1989: 11).

A child with good number sense will be able to tell you lots of facts about a number. For example, take the number 6. What do we know about 6? It is:

- 2×3
- half of 12
- 1 less than 7
- made up from $5 + 1$, $4 + 2$, $3 + 3$

- an even number
- a factor of 24.

Children with poor number sense will find the above very hard as they don't really understand the concept of 6, sometimes referred to as the 'sixness of six', and they don't understand how 6 relates to other numbers. So children with poor number sense find it hard to develop meaning for numbers and operations. They don't look for relationships and connections among numbers and operations and they don't have any flexibility in the way that they use numbers (Wilson and Dehaene 2007).

An inability to consider whether a numerical answer is reasonable

Most children are reluctant to estimate an answer before they calculate it, but a dyscalculic learner will have no concept of whether the answer they have calculated is reasonable or not. This inability to estimate persists into adulthood (Mejias et al. 2011).

Immature strategies

Dyscalculic learners tend to cling on to procedures that they feel secure with, for example, counting all instead of counting on when adding two numbers. They don't have the confidence to play with the numbers or to try out new, more efficient methods. In this respect, they often end up doing a harder, more laborious form of maths, as they will apply long-winded and inefficient procedures instead of seeing a quicker, more elegant route to the answer (Geary et al. 1991).

An inability to notice patterns

Our brains are wired up to notice patterns – it is the way that we make sense of the world. Learners with dyscalculia find this very difficult, as they are unable to easily spot the patterns in maths. Being able to see patterns in maths makes it much easier for us to generalize and to predict solutions. Ashkenazi et al. (2013) studied the ability of children with developmental dyscalculia to subitize and found that even when the dots were canonically arranged (i.e. in a regular pattern), there was still a deficit in their subitizing ability compared with their non-dyscalculic peers.

An inability to generalize

Generalizing is all about being able to transfer acquired knowledge to a novel situation. The ability to do this helps us to make sense of maths and to understand the connections and patterns. Dyscalculic learners struggle with generalization of ideas and concepts and find it hard to transfer information from one area of maths to another. Consequently, for these learners, maths is a multitude of individual pieces of information that have to be stored and remembered or calculated from first principles every time.

Delay in counting

Dyscalculic learners show a marked delay in counting and have difficulty understanding counting principles such as cardinality and one-to-one correspondence (Geary et al. 1992). They tend to persist in using immature counting strategies.

Difficulty recalling tables and number facts

Ginsburg (1997) found that dyscalculic learners have marked difficulty remembering arithmetical facts such as times tables and number bonds. This makes it much harder for them to carry out simple calculations, particularly if they have to do them mentally.

Difficulty processing number symbols

Dyscalculic learners find it difficult to match the number symbol to the physical numerical quantity (Rousselle and Nocl 2007). The areas of the brain where these two pieces of information are stored are completely separate. Number symbols are processed in the inferior temporal gyrus (Parvizi et al. 2013) while numerical quantity is processed in the intraparietal sulcus (Hyde et al. 2010).

Difficulty finger counting

Young children use their fingers to help them to learn basic maths principles. However, it is hotly debated whether finger-based representations are beneficial or detrimental. From a neurocognitive point of view, there are research data to show that children with good 'finger sense' have better numerical skill than those who do not. Finger training to develop this number sense has been seen to benefit these children in terms of their numerical development. However, some quarters in maths education believe that children should be weaned off finger use and encouraged to represent the maths with concrete materials before moving on to abstract mental calculations (Moeller et al. 2011).

Dyscalculic learners find it hard to use their fingers to support calculations and are often slow, inaccurate, and unable to immediately recognize finger configurations. Boaler and Chen (2016) recommend finger training activities to help support children in their numerical development.

Difficulty decomposing numbers

Dyscalculic learners find it very hard to break numbers up into smaller parts – for example, recognizing that 10 is made up of 4 and 6, 7 and 3, 8 and 2, etc. Sharma (2015) compares this to phonemic awareness. The ability to break words into meaningful chunks and blend chunks fluently back together is a predictor of early reading performance. In a similar way, the ability to decompose and recompose number can be seen as a precursor to numerical development. Learners without this sense of how numbers are constructed will struggle to develop fluency in mathematical thinking.

How to identify children with dyscalculia

There is no single test for dyscalculia and the complexity of this specific learning difficulty does not lend itself to easy diagnosis. However, a range of tools and assessments is available that can help to build a picture of an individual's strengths and weaknesses in order to conclude whether their difficulties are of a dyscalculic nature or not. These include:

- Checklists
- Screening tools
- Observation and error analysis
- Informal assessment
- Full diagnostic assessment.

Checklists

Checklists are simple and quick to administer and are often the option of choice when trying to identify dyscalculia. However, they can be very subjective and will only ever give an indication of whether the learner is at risk of dyscalculia.

Many checklists for dyscalculia can either be purchased or accessed free online, including:

● The British Dyslexia Association Checklist for Dyscalculia [www.bdadyslexia.org].
● Ann Arbor Dyscalculia Checklist [www.annarbor.co.uk].
● More Trouble with Maths by Steve Chinn includes a 31-point checklist [www.stevechinn.co.uk].
● The Mathematics Shed has a more comprehensive checklist that is divided into the following areas: number system, calculations, solving problems, measures, shape and space and handling data [www.mathematicshed.com].

Screening tools

The next step after completing a checklist would be to administer a dyscalculia screening tool. There are only a few of these available at present.

Numeracy Screener [www.numeracyscreener.org]

Researchers at the University of Western Ontario have developed a two-minute screening test to identify children aged 4–8 years who are struggling. These children may just need extra support or they may have specific learning difficulties. The test itself will not be able to identify dyscalculia as such, but it will highlight those children who may need extra input or more careful monitoring. The test is free and very easy to administer. It can be downloaded at numeracyscreener. org, together with test instructions. The children are required to identify which of two numbers or symbols is larger on a series of worksheets. They answer as many questions as they can in two minutes.

Dynamo Maths Profiler [www.dynamoprofiler.co.uk]

This screening tool was developed by Dynamo Maths, a company offering online intervention activities for learners with dyscalculia and maths difficulties. The Dynamo Maths Profiler is a simple online test that will identify specific areas of difficulty, in particular individual variation in number sense development. It is aimed at children aged 6–9 years and takes between 20 and 40 minutes to complete. It covers:

- Speed of processing
- Number meaning
- Number relationships
- Number magnitude.

This screener is particularly useful because it produces two reports: the Number Sense Profile Report distinguishes between dyscalculic difficulties and developmental delay in maths, while the Performance Profile Report gives a detailed view of the child's strengths and weaknesses and signposts intervention strategies to support them. The results are displayed in bar chart format.

Cost: £24.99 plus VAT per individual administration.

The Dyscalculia Screener [www.gl-assessment.co.uk]

This screening tool was developed by Brian Butterworth, Professor of Cognitive Neuropsychology at University College London. The screener identifies dyscalculic tendencies in children aged 6–14 years and provides a report that recommends intervention strategies for support. An accompanying book, *Dyscalculia Guidance*, is available that details games and activities for such intervention strategies. The test takes around 30 minutes to complete and can be used individually or as a whole-class screener. It aims to help practitioners distinguish between individuals who have poor maths attainment and those whose difficulties are associated with dyscalculia. It assesses the learner's sense of number through evaluating their ability to understand number size and how well they perform simple calculations.

Cost: £5.50 plus VAT per individual administration (for a minimum of 10 administrations).

DyscalculiUM [www.dyscalculia.advancelearningzone.com]

DyscalculiUM is a screener for older learners (aged 16+) developed by Clare Trott at Loughborough University. It can be used individually or for large groups and takes less than an hour to complete. The screener aims to assess understanding of basic number sense and how to apply number concepts to everyday situations. A profile of strengths and weaknesses is produced along with recommendations for support.

The DyscalculiUM tool assesses performance in six key areas:

● Number Conceptual
● Number Comparative
● Graphical
● Symbolic Abstraction
● Spatial Temporal
● Operational.

Cost: £9.95 per individual administration (for a minimum of 20 administrations).

Observation and error analysis

As well as more formal ways of assessing maths difficulties, one of the most informative can be through observation and error analysis. This can provide insight into the misconceptions that a learner has, their cognitive processing, and the strategies that they use. The key here is to sit with the learner while they complete a range of questions and ask them to verbalize their thought processes while attempting to work out the answers. Many learners find it hard to explain their thinking but careful questioning can help them to unpick their thoughts. This provides insight into their level of understanding. Although it may be tempting, try not to correct them when they make a mistake, but do ask them to explain their thinking and why they have come up with that particular answer. Observation and error analysis such as this can give you a good idea where learners' difficulties stem from and also whether they are down to gaps in knowledge and common misconceptions, or the difficulties are more fundamental and due to dyscalculia.

Informal assessment

There are a couple of books that can be very helpful in building a more detailed profile of a learner's difficulties with maths.

The first is *The Dyscalculia Assessment* (2013) by Jane Emerson and Patricia Babtie. This very useful book will help practitioners to identify which aspects of numeracy the child is struggling to acquire. The evidence from the assessment can then be used to draw up a personalized teaching plan. It is ideal for use with primary school children but can also be adapted for use with older children.

The book is written in a very clear way with step-by-step instructions and assessment sheets for photocopying that help in formulating individual intervention programmes. It contains guidance on how to conduct the assessments, including suggested scripts, teaching tips and strategies, as well as instructions on interpretation of the results and a range of motivating games and activities.

The second book is *More Trouble with Maths* (2017) by Steve Chinn. This is a highly practical, easy-to-use book that covers assessment of a wide range of factors. Steve Chinn draws on his extensive experience and expertise to:

- show you how to consider all the factors relating to mathematical learning difficulties;
- explain how these factors can be investigated;
- explore their impact on learning;
- discuss and provide a range of tests ranging from pre-requisite skills such as working memory to a critique of normative tests for mathematics knowledge and skills.

The book guides the reader in the interpretation of tests, emphasizing the need for a clinical approach when assessing individuals, and shows how diagnosis and assessment can become part of everyday teaching. This resource also includes pragmatic tests that can be implemented in the classroom, and shows how identifying the barriers must be the first step in setting up any programme of intervention.

It includes the following:

- Dyscalculia checklist
- Observation sheet
- Short-term and working memory test
- 60 second test for addition and subtraction
- 120 second test for multiplication and division
- Maths anxiety assessment

- 15 minute maths test
- Test of cognitive style in maths
- Word problems.

Full diagnostic assessment

A full diagnostic assessment for dyscalculia can be carried out by a specialist assessor or an educational psychologist. A range of standardized tests will need to be administered in order to ascertain whether the underlying difficulty is indeed dyscalculia or whether there is a different cause. Tests to assess verbal and visual IQ, working memory, and processing speed should all be administered. These quantitative assessments need to be interpreted alongside more qualitative assessments so that a complete picture of the learner's profile can be built up. For example, factors such as maths anxiety, educational history, family history, and developmental milestones should be considered.

It is worth bearing in mind the cost of these assessments and the potential benefit to the child. A full dyscalculia diagnosis can be a lengthy and costly exercise. Many learners will respond well to a high-quality, specifically tailored intervention from suitably qualified teachers. So, as long as the learner's strengths and weaknesses have been recognized, it should be possible to plan a detailed intervention programme that will meet their specific needs. If extra time will help, then a diagnostic assessment would be useful in applying for extra time in statutory exams, particularly if the child has poor processing speed.

A table of approved psychometric tests is given in the appendix to this book. Recommended maths assessments include:

Key Maths 3

The Key Maths 3 assessment and instruction system assesses maths skills of learners aged 4 1/2 to 21 years. This is a comprehensive system that consists of three linked components:

- Diagnostic assessment
- Scoring and reporting software
- Essential resources instructional program, which provides two levels of instruction for Key Stage 1 and Key Stage 2.

The diagnostic assessment is an untimed, norm-referenced, individually administered test. It has two parallel forms. The items are grouped into 10 subtests that represent three general math content areas:

- Basic concepts (conceptual knowledge)
- Operations (computational skills)
- Applications (problem-solving).

Sandwell Numeracy Tests

These are two highly regarded and commonly administered tests:

- The Sandwell Early Numeracy Test Revised (SENT-R) is a standardized test for children aged 4–8 years. It enables practitioners to assess children's ability with numbers, through exploring five strands of basic number skills: identification, oral counting, value, object counting, and language. The test needs to be administered on a one-to-one basis as it is an oral test and will provide a starting point for developing teaching programmes and specific interventions.
- The Sandwell Early Numeracy Test Key Stage 2 and 3 follows on from the SENT-R and covers the age range 9–16 years. It assesses children's ability in the same five strands as the SENT-R and provides diagnostic information upon which interventions can be planned.

Hodder Maths Competency test

This is a quick and convenient measure of mathematics skills and attainment, giving a skills profile as well as a norm-referenced total score. It provides questions sampled from four key areas of mathematics: Using & Applying Mathematics; Number & Algebra; Space & Shape; Handling Data – and uses open-ended questions, presented in ascending order of difficulty. It covers an age range of 11 years to adulthood.

References

American Psychiatric Association (APA) (2000) *Diagnostic and Statistical Manual of Mental Disorders* (4th edn.) (DSM-IV). Washington, DC: APA.

American Psychiatric Association (APA) (2013) *Diagnostic and Statistical Manual of Mental Disorders* (5th edn.) (DSM-V). Washington, DC: APA.

Ashkenazi, S., Mark-Zigdon, N. and Henik, A. (2013) Do subitizing deficits in developmental dyscalculia involve pattern recognition weakness?, *Developmental Science*, 16(1): 35–46.

Attwood, T. (2012) Retrieved from: www.dyscalculia.me.uk (accessed 11 September 2016).

Boaler, J. and Chen, L. (2016) Why kids should use their fingers in maths class, *The Atlantic* [retrieved from: https://www.theatlantic.com/education/archive/2016/04/why-kids-should-use-their-fingers-in-math-class/478053/; accessed 18 March 2017].

British Dyslexia Association (BDA) (2017) *Dyscalculia* [retrieved from: www.bdadyslexia.org.uk/dyslexic/dyscalculia; accessed 23 May 2017].

Butterworth, B. (2005a) Developmental dyscalculia, in J.I.D. Campbell (ed.) *Handbook of Mathematical Cognition* (pp. 455–67). Hove: Psychology Press.

Butterworth, B. (2005b) The development of arithmetical abilities, *Journal of Child Psychology and Psychiatry*, 46(1): 3–18.

Castelli, F., Glaser, D. and Butterworth, B. (2006) Discrete analogue quantity processing in the parietal lobe: a functional MRI study, *Proceedings of the National Academy of Sciences USA*, 103(12): 4693–8.

Chinn, S. (2017) *More Trouble with Maths* (2nd edn.). Abingdon: Routledge.

Dehaene, S. (2011) *The Number Sense: How the mind creates mathematics*. New York: Oxford University Press.

Department for Education (DfE) (2014) *National Curriculum*. London: DfE.

Department for Education and Science (DfES) (2001) *Guidance to Support Pupils with Dyslexia and Dyscalculia*. London: DfES Publications.

Emerson, J. and Babtie, P. (2013) *The Dyscalculia Assessment*. London: Bloomsbury.

Eves, H. (1987) *Return to Mathematical Circles: A fifth collection of mathematical stories and anecdotes*. Boston, MA: PWS-Kent.

Geary, D., Brown, S. and Samaranayake, V. (1991) Cognitive addition: a short longitudinal study of strategy choice and speed-of-processing differences in normal and mathematically disabled children, *Developmental Psychology*, 27: 787–97.

Geary, D., Bow-Thomas, C. and Yao, Y. (1992) Counting knowledge and skill in cognitive addition: a comparison of normal and mathematically disabled children, *Journal of Experimental Child Psychology*, 54(3): 372–91.

Gersten, R. and Chard, D. (1999) Number sense: rethinking arithmetic instruction for students with mathematical disabilities, *Journal of Special Education*, 33(1): 118–28.

Ginsburg, H. (1997) Mathematics learning disabilities: a view from developmental psychology, *Journal of Learning Disabilities*, 30(1): 20–33.

Howden, H. (1989) Teaching number sense, *Arithmetic Teacher*, 36(6): 6–11.

Hyde, D., Boas, D., Blair, C. and Carey, S. (2010) Near-infrared spectroscopy shows right parietal specialisation for number in pre-verbal infants, *NeuroImage*, 53(2): 647–52.

Isaacs, E., Edmonds, C., Lucas, A. and Gadian, D. (2001) Calculation difficulties in children of very low birthweight: a neural correlate, *Brain: A Journal of Neurology*, 124(9): 1701–7.

Jackson, M. and Warrington, E. (1986) Arithmetic skills in patients with unilateral cerebral lesions, *Cortex*, 22(4): 611–20.

Karagiannakis, G. and Cooreman, A. (2015) Focused MLD intervention based on the classification of MLD subtypes, in S. Chinn (ed.) *The Routledge International Handbook of Dyscalculia and Mathematical Learning Difficulties* (pp. 265–7). Abingdon: Routledge.

Kaufmann, L., Mazzocco, M.M., Dowker, A., von Aster, M., Göbel, S.M., Grabner, R.H. et al. (2013) Dyscalculia from a developmental and differential perspective, *Frontiers in Psychology*, 4: 516.

Klein, A. and Starkey, P. (1988) Universals in the development of early arithmetic cognition, in G.B. Saxe and M. Gearhart (eds.) *Children's Mathematics* (pp. 5–26). San Francisco, CA: Jossey-Bass.

Kosc, L. (1974) Developmental dyscalculia, *Journal of Learning Disabilities*, 7(3): 164–77.

Mejias, S., Gregiore, J. and Noel, M. (2011) Numerical estimation in adults with and without developmental dyscalculia, *Learning and Individual Differences*, 22(1): 164–70.

Moeller, K., Martignon, L., Wessolowski, S., Engel, J. and Nuerk, H. (2011) Effects of finger counting on numerical development: the opposing views of neurocognition and mathematics education, *Frontiers in Psychology*, 2: 328.

Murphy, M., Mazzocco, M., Gerner, G. and Henry, A. (2006) Mathematics learning disability in girls with Turner syndrome or fragile X syndrome, *Brain and Cognition*, 61(2): 195–210.

Muter, V. (2013) Dyslexia: Why more than one difficulty? How multiple deficit models influence assessment and intervention, in *Patoss Summer 2013 Bulletin*.

Parvizi, J., Shum, J., Hermes, D., Foster, B., Dastjerdi, M., Rangarajan, V. et al. (2013) A brain area for visual numerals, *Journal of Neurosciences*, 33(16): 6709–15.

Price, G. and Ansari, D. (2013) Dyscalculia: characteristics, causes and treatments, *Numeracy*, 6(1): art. 2.

Rousselle, L. and Noel, M.-P. (2007) Basic numerical skills in children with mathematics learning disabilities: a comparison of symbolic vs. non-symbolic number magnitude processing, *Cognition*, 102(3): 361–95.

Shalev, R. and Gross-Tsur, V. (2001) Developmental dyscalculia, *Paediatric Neurology*, 24(5): 337–42.

Sharma, M. (1997) *Dyscalculia* [retrieved from: www.webcitation.org/5a5tLlpxE; accessed 22 May 2017].

Sharma, M. (2015) Numbersense: a window into dyscalculia and other mathematical difficulties, in S. Chinn (ed.) *The Routledge International Handbook of Dyscalculia and Mathematical Difficulties* (pp. 277–91). Abingdon: Routledge.

Skagerlund, K. and Traff, U. (2016) Number processing and heterogeneity of developmental dyscalculia: subtypes with different cognitive profiles and deficits, *Journal of Learning Disabilities*, 49(1): 36–50.

Thambirajah, M.S. (2011) *Developmental Assessment of the School-aged Child with Developmental Disabilities*. London: Jessica Kingsley Publishers.

Wilson, A.J. and Dehaene, S. (2007) Number sense and developmental dyscalculia, in D. Coch, G. Dawson and K. Fischer (eds.) *Human Behaviour, Learning and the Developing Brain: Atypical development* (pp. 212–38). New York: Guilford Press.

Dyslexia

> Dyslexics think differently, they are intuitive and excel at problem solving, seeing the big picture and simplifying. They are poor reciters but inspired visionaries.
>
> Sally Shaywitz (2005: 366)

The word 'dyslexia' originates from Greek and literally means 'difficulty with words'. It affects around 10% of the population and is a genetic, inherited, lifelong condition. Dyslexia is not related to intelligence and occurs in people from all nationalities. Dyslexia was first identified by Dr Pringle-Morgan in 1896, in an article in the *British Medical Journal* describing a 14-year-old boy called Percy. He could 'only with difficulty spell out words of one syllable', wrote his name as 'Precy', and 'did not notice the mistake until his attention was called to it more than once' (Pringle Morgan 1896: 1378).

Furthermore, his teacher commented that if the classes had been entirely oral in nature, Percy would have been the smartest child in the school. We know from this historical account that dyslexia is unrelated to intelligence. Alarmingly, for many years learners with dyslexia have felt that they are 'stupid' or have been thought of as 'lazy', when we have known since the end of the twentieth century that this is not the case.

Dyslexia does occur across all nationalities, but to differing extents, depending on the orthography of the native language. The effects of dyslexia are exacerbated if the language of the dyslexic individual has deep orthography (Spencer 2000). Studies of Italian-speaking and English-speaking dyslexic children have revealed similar brain differences on MRI scans (Paulesu et al. 2001) but the Italian children struggle less with literacy due to the transparent nature of the Italian language. Italian is more transparent than English because it has fewer phonemes. Words tend to be pronounced the way that they are spelt, unlike English, which has multiple pronunciations of the same letter strings– for example, bough, dough, rough, cough, and through.

Dyslexia often co-occurs with other learning difficulties, such as dyspraxia and attention deficit hyperactivity disorder (ADHD) (Deponio 2004). It also frequently co-occurs with dyscalculia (Butterworth and Kovas 2013), with a higher than expected level of co-occurrence between these two specific learning difficulties, although the areas of the brain associated with dyslexia and dyscalculia are completely separate. Like dyslexic learners, dyscalculics often have difficulty retrieving facts from memory.

What is dyslexia?

There is no single definition of dyslexia, but many practitioners choose to refer to the Rose Review definition. In 2009, the government commissioned Sir Jim Rose to carry out a review on provision in UK schools for children with dyslexia and literacy difficulties. The resulting report offered the following definition of dyslexia:

> Dyslexia is a learning difficulty that primarily affects the skills involved in accurate and fluent word reading and spelling. Characteristic features of dyslexia are difficulties in phonological awareness, verbal memory and verbal processing speed. Dyslexia occurs across a range of intellectual abilities. It is best thought of as a continuum, not a distinct category, and there are no clear cut-off points. Co-occurring difficulties may be seen in aspects of language, motor co-ordination, mental calculation, concentration and personal organisation, but these are not, by themselves, markers of dyslexia. A good indication of the severity and persistence of dyslexic difficulties can be gained by examining how the individual responds or has responded to well founded intervention.
>
> (Rose 2009: 9–10)

The British Dyslexia Association (BDA) welcomed this 'working definition' but felt that there needed to be acknowledgement of the difficulties of a visual processing nature that some individuals with dyslexia can experience. It also wanted to emphasize the positive aspects of dyslexia.

> Individuals who experience dyslexia have learning differences and can show a combination of abilities and difficulties that affect the learning process. Some learners have strengths in other areas, such as design, problem solving, creative skills, interactive skills and oral skills.
>
> (BDA 2014)

Dyslexia Action has offered the following definition that highlights particular aspects and refers to differences in brain structure:

> Dyslexia is a specific learning difficulty that mainly affects reading and spelling. Dyslexia is characterised by difficulties in processing word-sounds and by weaknesses in short-term verbal memory; its effects may be seen in spoken language as well as written language. The current evidence suggests that these difficulties arise from inefficiencies in language-processing areas in the left hemisphere of the brain which, in turn, appear to be linked to genetic differences.
>
> (Dyslexia Action 2006)

Gavin Reid offers a useful definition, focusing on dyslexia as a learning difference:

> Dyslexia is a processing difference, often characterized by difficulties in literacy acquisition affecting reading, writing and spelling. It can also have an impact on cognitive processes such as memory, speed of processing, time management, co-ordination and automaticity. There may be visual and/or phonological difficulties and there are usually some discrepancies in educational performances.
>
> (Reid 2008)

Common themes

Some common themes can be identified from all of the above definitions:

- Dyslexia affects the ability to learn to read and spell.
- Dyslexic learners have difficulty processing and manipulating the sounds in words, which can make it hard for them to use phonics when learning to read.

- It can affect memory, in terms of how information is both stored in, and retrieved from, memory.
- There is no 'typical' dyslexic profile. Dyslexia can be mild or severe and people with dyslexia will have a variety of spiky profiles with some areas of strength and other areas of weakness.
- Dyslexia is unrelated to intelligence, but it is hereditary.
- Dyslexia is a lifelong condition but can be alleviated by good quality intervention and many people learn strategies to help them to manage the effects of their dyslexia.
- Dyslexia often co-occurs with other specific learning difficulties such as dyspraxia, ADHD, and dyscalculia.

Dyslexia indicators

Dyslexic learners have a distinct pattern of weaknesses and strengths that are underpinned by three main cognitive difficulties:

- Phonological deficit
- Memory
- Processing speed.

Each of these has an impact on how effectively we can learn. Learning involves three main processes: encoding (taking in information), storage (holding and organizing information), and retrieval (recalling stored information). These cognitive differences will lead to a variety of dyslexic indicators, with some areas of weakness and some areas of strength.

Weaknesses

Difficulty learning to read

This is the main area of difficulty that is associated with dyslexia, and it is the case that most dyslexic children will find it hard to learn to read. This difficulty is exacerbated if they are under pressure, for example, by having to read in public. However, many children develop strategies to overcome this difficulty and it is not uncommon for dyslexia to go 'under the radar' until learners enter further or higher education, when the sheer volume of reading overwhelms them.

For many children, it is the language demands of maths that are the barrier to their learning. Reading and understanding word problems can be challenging, even if they can actually do the maths. Words with multiple meanings can also cause confusion, such as 'product' and 'table'.

Difficulty learning to spell

Dyslexic learners often have very inconsistent spelling, sometimes misspelling the same word in several different ways in one piece of writing. They can also use very bizarre and seemingly illogical spellings. In my experience, spelling difficulties tend to persist into adulthood.

Difficulty processing information at speed

It can take a lot longer for a dyslexic learner to process information. This may be because of short-term or working memory issues or it may be that the cerebellum, which is at the back of the brain, is not functioning properly. There is often an undue emphasis on speed in maths, where answering quickly is equated to being capable in maths. For learners with poor processing speed this can be very challenging, as they need more time to process the information and to perform mental and written calculations. Research has shown that, on average, teachers will give children 1.5 seconds to answer a question (Rowe 1972).

The cerebellum is the part of the brain that controls actions that are performed automatically, without conscious thought, such as reading, walking, and writing (Fawcett and Nicolson 2008). If the cerebellum is unable to function efficiently, these tasks are taken up by the frontal lobe, which is where higher-order thinking takes place and this can slow down the working of the frontal lobe quite considerably.

Procedural learning can be defined as learning how to do something to the point where it is automatic. You can do it without having to think about it. The process of learning to automaticity is much more difficult if you're dyslexic.

The implication of this for maths learning is clear, as many dyslexic learners will have difficulty automatically applying procedures and algorithms.

Difficulty in retaining information in short-term/working memory

For many dyslexic learners, the encoding, storage, and retrieval of information can be very problematic. They may have difficulty in holding information in their short-term memory, or in transferring it to their long-term memory, or in retrieving it from memory.

Short-term and working memory have a limited capacity, with most people only being able to store around seven pieces of unrelated information, for about 30 seconds. This is sometimes referred to as our 'memory shelf'. If too many items are put onto the memory shelf, something will fall off. For dyslexic learners, this memory shelf can be very small, with maybe only the capacity for three or four items. Also, for some learners, if the shelf is overloaded it can collapse, leading to a 'catastrophic memory loss' (Gathercole et al. 2006), where an individual is unable to recall information. It may be the case that the information has been lost before the learner has had the chance to act upon it. Learners with this difficulty often give the appearance of not having listened to a word that the teacher has said, whereas in fact they have just been overloaded with information and have lost everything.

This can be particularly problematic in maths when learners are attempting multi-step problems or mental calculations, which require multiple items of information to be stored and manipulated.

Difficulty transferring information into long-term memory

One characteristic trait of a learner with dyslexia that can be very frustrating for all concerned is their inability to transfer information into their long-term memory. These learners appear to have 'got it' in the lesson but when the area of learning is revisited, it will often have all but disappeared. This can manifest itself in children being unable to learn times tables or number facts, as the information has only been temporarily stored in their short-term memory.

Word retrieval problems: tip of the tongue syndrome

This is a typical dyslexic-type problem and stems from language-processing difficulties (Murphy et al. 1988). Often, the dyslexic learner knows what word they want to use but find it hard to retrieve it from their long-term memory. The same is true for maths facts and procedures. The learner may know that the information is 'in there somewhere', but can have great difficulty retrieving it.

Inability to identify some sounds in words

Phonological processing refers to how well we can identify and manipulate individual sounds in words. It is a key skill in being able to read and one that dyslexic learners have great difficulty with. They will often employ compensatory strategies such as relying on visual and semantic cues to help them overcome their phonological weaknesses. Due to their poor phonological awareness, dyslexic learners often have difficulty isolating individual sounds in words. For example, they may not hear the 'n' in 'strand' and this can make it very hard for them to spell words correctly. Problems may exist with auditory or visual discrimination and perception. Poor auditory perception and discrimination will make it hard to perceive the difference between similar sounds, such as (ĕ) and (ĭ), and this will lead to difficulties when reading and spelling.

Mismatch between oral and written work

Dyslexic learners are often very articulate, with a large vocabulary. However, they find it hard to translate this to their written work. One child described this as 'the words in my mind are not the same as the words in my hand or at least in my pen'.

Tracking difficulties

Some, but not all, dyslexic learners may have tracking difficulties. This means that their eyes do not fixate as they move over words on a page. This has clear implications for maths learning, as it may be very hard for the learner to keep track of which calculation on the page they are working on. This can easily be remedied by the use of aperture cards. These cards have a small window cut out of them, so that they can be placed over a page of calculations ensuring that only one calculation is seen at a time.

Visual stress

Poor visual perception can lead to difficulties in discriminating between similar letters, such as 'b' and 'd' or 'p' and 'q', or between symbols used in maths, such as '+' and '×'.

Some people see this as a separate issue from dyslexia, whereas others see it as part and parcel of a dyslexic profile. The indicators of this difficulty include:

- letters or numbers which move, or jump around the page;
- blurred or fuzzy letters/numbers;
- headaches when reading;
- double vision or gaps between letters in words;
- difficulty reading small, tightly spaced text, or elaborate scripts;
- easily losing one's place on a page and difficulty tracking across a page;
- oversensitivity to bright lights or to black text on a white background.

Moeller et al. (2009) investigated whether tracking difficulties were the cause of dyscalculic learners' inability to subitize. Certainly, visual stress can cause problems when extracting numerical information from tables and graphs.

Letter/digit reversal

This is a common stage of development, but for a dyslexic learner this difficulty will persist long after normal developmental stages. The most common letters to be reversed are those whose lower cases are very similar, namely, p/q, b/d, m/n, and i/j. Often a dyslexic learner will substitute the capital forms of these letters within words, as it is easier for them to distinguish the capital form. For example, writing 'I went to BeD' instead of 'I went to bed'. Digits can also be easily reversed, as some are formed in a clockwise direction and some in an anticlockwise direction.

Clockwise digits: 1, 2, 3, 7

Anticlockwise digits: 0, 4, 5, 6, 8, 9

Time management: organization and sequencing

As dyslexic learners get older, it is often organization that becomes the issue rather than reading or spelling. Dyslexic teenagers have many demands at secondary school with regards to which books they need for a particular day. Many secondary schools operate on a two-week timetable and this can be particularly challenging.

Illegible handwriting

Not all dyslexic learners have poor handwriting, and if they do then it tends to be due to dyspraxia or dysgraphia, but some learners deliberately foster a messy handwriting style to mask their poor spelling. In terms of maths this can lead to difficulties in setting out calculations correctly, leading to errors caused by misaligning columns or misreading individual numbers.

Left/right confusion

This is a very common indicator of dyslexia, and again is something that many young children struggle with. The difference for a dyslexic learner is that left/right confusion persists. This is often coupled with letter reversals or mirror writing.

Another thing to look out for here is cross-laterality. Generally speaking, if you are left handed you will be left footed, left eyed, and left eared, but people with cross-laterality have a mixture of left and right. This forms one of the subtests on the Aston Index, a dyslexia assessment originally devised in the 1970s but which has since been updated (Newton 2003). It is straightforward to replicate this test with a few simple props. To test for footedness, put a football on the floor in front of the child and see what foot they naturally kick it with. To test for which eye is dominant, ask the child to look though a cardboard tube and see which eye they put the tube to. To test for the dominant ear, place a ticking watch on the table and ask them to pick it up and see if they can hear the tick, and make a note of which ear they put the watch to.

Learners with cross-laterality are more likely to have left/right confusion and may struggle in maths, as some procedures go from left to right and others from right to left.

Left to right:

$$23) \overline{460}$$

Right to left:

$$\begin{array}{r} 236 \\ + 460 \\ \hline \end{array}$$

Having to work much harder than other children

Dyslexic learners have to put in much more effort than their non-dyslexic peers. This can be due to poor processing speed or poor functioning of the cerebellum. It is believed that a dyslexic learner can work five times as hard as someone without dyslexia (Richards et al. 1999).

Low self-esteem

Many dyslexic children suffer from low self-esteem and a lack of self-confidence, particularly if they are not aware of their dyslexia or if they have not received appropriate support (Humphrey and Mullins 2002). This can be a very significant barrier in terms of academic achievement, as maths is a subject that is very susceptible to fragile self-esteem. Learners who are confident in maths are much more likely to attempt difficult questions and are more likely to work at the edge of their comfort zone. In contrast, learners who have no confidence in their maths ability will be reluctant to take risks and will tend to work well within their comfort zone, and therefore will be less likely to make good progress in maths.

Copying from the board

Dyslexic learners find it very hard to copy from the board and this should be avoided at all costs. You can spot this difficulty because the dyslexic learner will frequently lose their place and will constantly be looking up to the board and back to the paper, much more than their peers. This can be a huge issue in maths, where many calculations may be displayed on the board at once. The dyslexic learner will find it very hard to keep track of which question they are answering and will often mix up parts of different questions.

History of poor reading/spelling

We know that dyslexia is hereditary, so it is highly likely that there will be a history of literacy difficulties in the family (Francks et al. 2002).

Strengths

The good news is that as well as this list of weaknesses, dyslexic learners have strengths also (Eide and Eide 2011), and these are being much more widely recognized in the workplace. Around 10% of the population is dyslexic, yet over 50% of NASA employees are reportedly dyslexic. They are said to be sought-after because they have superb problem-solving skills and excellent 3D and spatial awareness.

Creativity

Dyslexic individuals learn in a different way because they think in a different way and it is this difference that can make them so creative. They also often have to find different ways of overcoming their difficulties, so can be very original and creative in their approach to learning.

Problem-solving

Dyslexic people are more disposed to be able to perceive subtle patterns in systems or data and to look at problems from a different perspective. They are also very good at finding best-fit solutions to problems.

Being able to see the 'big picture'

The brains of dyslexics are structured differently and dyslexic learners often excel at seeing the gist or essence of a situation. They don't get bogged down by the detail and can spot the larger context behind ideas and situations, viewing things holistically rather than in minute detail.

Innovation

This can be a great strength for the dyslexic learner, as they can see novel or obscure connections, which helps them to be more innovative and creative in their thinking.

Three-dimensional spatial ability and visualization

Many dyslexic learners are very good at thinking in three dimensions and make very good architects, mechanics, engineers, and designers as a result of this ability. They tend to see the world in pictures in their heads rather than in words and have great visualization skills.

So, when you are looking for indicators of dyslexia in a learner, it is important to look for the strengths as well as the weaknesses, as they are all part of the dyslexic profile.

How to identify children with dyslexia

In terms of more formal identification, there are checklists, screening tools, and psychometric tests that can be administered to provide a more detailed standardized assessment of the child's difficulties.

Checklists

Checklists can be a useful starting point when moving towards a more formal identification of dyslexia. As always, they need to be treated with a certain degree of caution, as they can be very subjective.

- The British Dyslexia Association has checklists on its website for all ages of learner, from pre-school through to adulthood [www.bdadyslexia.org.uk].
- The website for Ann Arbor Publishers – a longstanding supplier of tests and resources to psychologists, teachers, and parents – provides free downloadable checklists for a wide range of learning difficulties, including dyslexia [www.annarbor.co.uk].
- Dyslexia Action has produced two checklists, one for learners aged 7–11 years and the other for 12-year-olds through to adulthood [www.dyslexiaaction.org.uk].

Screening tools

There are several screening tools for dyslexia, some online and others pen and paper based. A few of the more commonly used ones are detailed below.

Dyslexia Screener [www.gl-assessment.co.uk]

The Dyslexia Screener identifies dyslexic tendencies in learners aged 5–16 years and recommends intervention strategies to help. It is a 30 minute online standardized test comprising six subtests with two assessments for three areas, namely: Ability, Attainment, and

Diagnostic. Two reports are generated, a diagnostic group report and a report for parents.

Cost: £5.70 plus VAT per individual administration (minimum of 10 administrations).

Dyslexia Quest [www.nessy.com]

This screening test is one of the most recent to be marketed, covering learners aged 5–7, 8–10, and 11–16 years and provides a snapshot of learning abilities linked to dyslexia. It is games based and tests memory and learning skills in six games. A computer-generated report is available.

Cost: £10 per child.

Dyslexia Portfolio [www.gl-assessment.co.uk]

The Dyslexia Portfolio is a standardized diagnostic assessment tool that follows on from the Dyslexia Screener. It offers a range of nine subtests, including phonological processing, that help identify pupils with dyslexia and other literacy learning difficulties in the context of literacy attainment. It is more comprehensive than other screening tools. The individual diagnostic assessment provides a profile of strengths and weaknesses that can be translated directly into an individual teaching plan, enabling specialist teachers to devise and implement a relevant and sensitive, multi-sensory intervention programme. It takes about 40 minutes to administer on a one-to-one basis.

Cost: £200 plus VAT.

Dyslexia Screening Test [www.pearsonclinical.co.uk]

This includes four different standardized screening tests covering learners from 5 years to adulthood: the Dyslexia Early Screening Test (DEST), the Dyslexia Screening Test-Junior (DST-J), the Dyslexia Screening Test-Secondary (DST-S), and the Dyslexia Adult Screening Test (DAST). These tests are individually administered and comprise 12 subtests (11 for the adult screener). The tests generate an 'at-risk' score for dyslexia, determining whether further in-depth testing should be undertaken. A profile of skills provides valuable information that can be used to guide in-school support.

Cost: £180 plus VAT.

Full diagnostic assessment

The next stage on from screening is to consider carrying out a full diagnostic assessment. This needs to be done by a specialist dyslexia assessor or by an educational psychologist. This is a much more comprehensive assessment that will involve the administration of a range of psychometric tests. A report will be produced that will detail individual strengths and difficulties and provide a conclusion as to whether the learner has dyslexia or not.

Such reports can be very useful for exam access arrangements and for providing evidence to support the need for individual intervention programmes.

A comprehensive diagnostic assessment will test the following areas:

- Verbal and non-verbal IQ
- Memory function: short-term verbal memory and working memory
- Phonological awareness
- Processing speed
- Word reading/text reading/comprehension
- Spelling
- Writing: speed, handwriting, fluency, and style
- Sequencing.

It will not always be necessary to carry out a full diagnostic assessment, but certainly carrying out some form of screening will help practitioners to understand a learner's strengths and weaknesses and will help them to identify the underlying cause of the learner's difficulty with maths.

References

British Dyslexia Association (BDA) (2014) *Definitions* [retrieved from: www.bdadyslexia.org.uk; accessed 15 September 2016].

Butterworth, B. and Kovas, Y. (2013) Understanding neurocognitive developmental disorders can improve education for all, *Science*, 340(6130): 300–5.

Deponio, P. (2004) The co-occurrence of specific learning difficulties: implications for identification and assessment, in G. Reid and A.J. Fawcett (eds.) *Dyslexia in Context: Research, policy and practice* (pp. 323–35). Chichester: Wiley.

Dyslexia Action (2006) Retrieved from: www.dyslexiaaction.org.uk (accessed 15 September 2016).

Eide, L. and Eide, F. (2011) *The Dyslexic Advantage*. London: Hay House.

Fawcett, A.J. and Nicolson, R.I. (2008) Dyslexia: the role of the cerebellum, in G. Reid and A.J. Fawcett (eds.) *Dyslexia in Context: Research, Policy and Practice* (pp. 13–22). Chichester: Wiley.

Francks, C., MacPhie, I.L. and Monaco, A.P. (2002) The genetic basis of dyslexia, *Lancet Neurology*, 1(8): 483–90.

Gathercole, S.E., Alloway, T.P., Willis, C. and Adams, A.M. (2006) Working memory in children with reading disabilities, *Journal of Experimental Child Psychology*, 93(3): 265–81.

Humphrey, N. and Mullins, P. (2002) Self-concept and self-esteem in developmental dyslexia, *Journal of Research in Special Educational Needs*, 2(2): 1–13.

Moeller, K., Neuburger, S., Kaufmann, L., Landerl, K. and Neurk, H.-C. (2009) Basic number processing deficits in developmental dyscalculia: evidence from eye tracking, *Cognitive Development*, 24(4): 371–86.

Murphy, L.A., Pollatsek, A. and Well, A.D. (1988) Developmental dyslexia and word retrieval deficits, *Brain and Language*, 35(1): 1–23.

Newton, M. (2003) *Aston Index: A classroom test for screening and diagnosis of language difficulties*. Cambridge: LDA.

Paulesu, E., Démonet, J.F., Fazio, F., McCrory, E., Chanoine, V. and Brunswick, N. et al. (2001) Dyslexia: cultural diversity and biological unity, *Science*, 291(5511): 2165–7.

Pringle Morgan, W. (1896) A case of congenital word blindness, *British Medical Journal*, 2(1871): 1378.

Reid, G. (2009) *Dyslexia: A practitioner's handbook* (4th edn.). Chichester: Wiley-Blackwell.

Reid, G. (2008) *Dyslexia Definition* [retrieved from: www.drgavinreid.com/free-resources/dyslexia/; accessed 18 March 2017].

Richards, T.L., Dager, S.R., Corina, D., Serafini, S., Heide, A.C., Steury, K. et al. (1999) Dyslexic children have abnormal brain lactate response to reading-related language tasks, *American Journal of Neuroradiology*, 20(8): 1393–8.

Rose, J. (2009) *Identifying and Teaching Children and Young People with Dyslexia and Literacy Difficulties* (The Rose Review) [retrieved from www.interventionsforliteracy.org.uk/assets/Uploads/The-Rose-Report-June-2009.pdf; accessed 22 May 2017].

Rowe, M. (1972) Wait-time and rewards as instructional variables: their influence in language, logic, and fate control. Paper presented at the annual meeting of the National Association for Research on Science Teaching, Chicago, IL.

Shaywitz, S.E. (2005) *Overcoming Dyslexia: A new and complete science-based program for reading problems at any level.* New York: Random House.

Spencer, K.A. (2000) Is English a dyslexic language?, *Dyslexia*, 6: 152–62.

Dyspraxia

Everyone is a genius. But if you judge a fish on its ability to climb a tree, it will live its whole life believing that it is stupid.

Albert Einstein

What is dyspraxia?

The term dyspraxia originates from Greek and literally means 'difficulty in carrying out an action'. Dyspraxia is a developmental disorder of the brain causing difficulty in activities requiring coordination and movement. It can be described as an impairment or immaturity of the organization of movement, or a lack of development in a person's ability to 'get our bodies to do what we want and when we want them to do it' (Ripley et al. 1997: 3). It can cause difficulty with both spatial and perceptual skills and can manifest itself in the following areas:

- Speech and language
- Handwriting and drawing (dysgraphia)
- Whole-body movements and coordination
- Physical play/activity.

Dyspraxia or Developmental Co-ordination Disorder (DCD)?

These terms can be quite confusing and are commonly used interchangeably. However, there is a distinction between the two. Dyspraxia is a subtype of DCD. It is a specific example of DCD and is predominantly a sensory-based difficulty. DCD is predominantly a motor-based difficulty. In practice the distinction is rarely made and either of these terms may be used.

The Dyspraxia Foundation (2017) defines dyspraxia as follows

> Dyspraxia, a form of developmental coordination disorder (DCD), is a common disorder affecting fine and/or gross motor coordination in children and adults. It may also affect speech. DCD is a lifelong condition, formally recognised by international organisations including the World Health Organization. DCD is distinct from other motor disorders such as cerebral palsy and stroke, and occurs across the range of intellectual abilities. Individuals may vary in how their difficulties present: these may change over time depending on environmental demands and life experiences. An individual's coordination difficulties may affect participation and functioning of everyday life skills in education, work and employment.

The DSM-V Diagnostic Criteria for Developmental Co-ordination Disorder is as follows:

> Motor performance that is substantially below expected levels, given the person's chronologic age and previous opportunities for skill acquisition. The poor motor performance may manifest as coordination problems, poor balance, clumsiness, dropping or bumping into things; marked delays in achieving developmental motor milestones (e.g., walking, crawling, sitting) or in the acquisition of basic motor skills (e.g., catching, throwing, kicking, running, jumping, hopping, cutting, coloring, printing, writing).
>
> (APA 2013: 315.4)

Common threads

Dyspraxia is clearly a complex specific learning difficulty but there are common threads running through these definitions. Dyspraxia is:

- a lifelong condition that can impede daily living;
- a result of fine or gross motor skill deficit that leads to the impairment of the organization of movement.

What happens in dyspraxia?

Dyspraxia is characterized by disorganized wiring of the brain leading to inconsistent interaction with the environment. There are many different ways in which dyspraxia can manifest itself. The variants that affect maths the most are difficulties with visual perception, spatial awareness, and visual sequential memory.

Visual perception

Visual perception relates to how the brain interprets information that is received through the eyes. Problems can arise from having difficulty in coordinating eye movement, tracking from left to right, hand–eye coordination, processing visual information at speed, and receiving correct visual information. These difficulties can have a huge impact on learning, as the vast majority of information in school lessons is presented visually.

Visual perception difficulties will impact on maths development (Pieters et al. 2012) because learners will find it hard to discriminate between different shapes and symbols, for example '×' and '+'. They may have difficulty in interpreting diagrams, tables, and graphs. Frequently, learners with visual perception problems will set their maths problems in a messy, unaligned way, leading to errors in calculations.

Spatial awareness

Spatial awareness relates to how well we perceive our body position in relation to other objects in the environment. Learners with dyspraxia often have problems with spatial awareness, as the brain does not provide them with the correct information regarding relative positions and proximity of objects around them. This can lead to children frequently bumping into things or falling over, as well as being unaware of personal space. In terms of maths development, these children will find it difficult to interpret geometrical figures. They have trouble placing numbers on a number line and drawing and interpreting graphs.

Visual sequential memory

Visual sequential memory relates to our ability to store information received through the eyes in the correct sequence. The area of the brain that is affected is the visuospatial working memory. This is important in terms of maths development, as we depend on our visuospatial memory in many areas of maths. For example, to solve a problem like $9 + 6 = 15$, we need to perceive how the numbers and symbols are placed in relation to each other on a page and how that placement affects how they approach the problem. We also need to be able to align numbers vertically for column methods of calculations.

Dyspraxia indicators

It is not easy to diagnose dyspraxia, as it can manifest itself in so many different ways. For children under the age of 16, the diagnosis will need to be made by medical professionals.

Early signs

The signs of dyspraxia can be evident from a very early age. Dyspraxic babies tend to be irritable and may have difficulty feeding. They may also show delay in reaching developmental milestones, such as being able to sit independently. Dyspraxic babies are also more likely to be 'bottom shufflers', missing out on the crawling stage. This is a trait that is also shared with some dyslexic children. Children who have missed out on the crawling stage by either bottom shuffling or going straight to walking have missed out on the development stage of 'crossing the central line', a step needed to develop coordination of the left- and right-hand sides of the brain.

Foundation Stage

By nursery or reception age, other symptoms may become apparent. These children may be very fidgety and unable to sit still. They may have trouble with gross motor skills, such as riding a bike or throwing and catching a ball. Fine motor skill difficulties may be present, such as difficulty in holding a pencil, folding paper or using scissors. The children tend to avoid fiddly construction toys and can be very messy, constantly spilling drinks or eating with their fingers instead of using a knife and fork. Dyspraxia used to be referred to as 'clumsy child syndrome' (Gubbay 1975), and these children will often bump into things and be unaware of others' personal space.

Key Stage 1

By Key Stage 1, there will be a noticeable difference from their peers. These children will have difficulty dressing and undressing for PE, poor concentration, and may have difficulty following verbal instructions. They may also be displaying sensitivity to noise and light, such as the strip lighting that is found in many classrooms. Socially, they may find it hard to relate to other children and may have difficulty making friends. Fine and gross motor skill difficulties will persist, with illegible handwriting and difficulty drawing and copying.

Key Stage 2

If the signs of dyspraxia have not been identified and addressed, then by Key Stage 2 the dyspraxic child is likely to be suffering from low self-esteem and may be isolated in the classroom. Their difficulties will be more noticeable and they are likely to be disaffected at school (Skinner and Piek 2001).

How to identify children with dyspraxia

If a parent or practitioner is concerned that a child may have dyspraxia, the first port of call will be the child's GP. The GP will then refer the child to relevant professionals who will work together to form a diagnosis. In order to diagnose dyspraxia, according to the DSM-V criteria, two specific criteria must be met:

1   The acquisition and execution of coordinated motor skills is substantially below that expected given the individual's chronological age and opportunity for skill learning and use, and that this significantly and persistently interferes with activities of daily living. (This assessment can be carried out by an occupational therapist, a physiotherapist or a speech and language difficulties therapist.)

2   The motor skill difficulties are not better explained by visual impairment, neurological disorder or another medical condition. (This assessment may be carried out by a paediatrician or paediatric neurologist. In some cases, it may be necessary to refer the child to an educational psychologist, particularly if there are complex needs such as co-occurring difficulties.)

References

American Psychiatric Association (APA) (2013) *Diagnostic and Statistical Manual of Mental Disorders* (5th edn.) (DSM-V). Washington, DC: APA.

Dyspraxia Foundation (2017) *What is Dyspraxia?* [retrieved from: http://dyspraxiafoundation.org.uk/about-dyspraxia/; accessed 20 April 2017].

Gubbay, S. (1975) *The Clumsy Child: A study of developmental apraxic and agnosic ataxia.* Philadelphia, PA: Saunders.

Pieters, S., Desoete, A., Roeyers, H., Vanderswalmen, R. and Van Waelvelde, H. (2012) Behind mathematical learning disabilities: what about visual perception and motor skills?, *Learning and Individual Differences*, 22(4): 498–504.

Ripley, K., Daines, B. and Barrett, J. (1997) *Dyspraxia: A guide for teachers and parents.* London: David Fulton.

Skinner, R.A. and Piek, J.P. (2001) Psychosocial implications of poor motor coordination in children and adolescents, *Human Movement Science*, 20(1/2): 73–94.

CHAPTER

Practical strategies

Truth is ever to be found in the simplicity, and not in the multiplicity and confusion of things.

Isaac Newton

Having considered how to define and identify dyscalculia, dyslexia, and dyspraxia, this chapter will look at strategies to help overcome these specific learning difficulties. The chapter will address four distinct areas – core number, reasoning, memory, and visual spatial awareness – as these are the four main areas of difficulty for learners with dyscalculia (core number and reasoning), dyslexia (memory), and dyspraxia (visual spatial awareness).

DYSCALCULIA: STRATEGIES TO IMPROVE CORE NUMBER AND REASONING

One of the main ways to address any difficulty with core number and reasoning is to develop number sense.

What is number sense?

The importance of number sense in maths development was highlighted by Gersten and Chard (1999): 'Just as our understanding of phonemic awareness has revolutionized the teaching of beginning reading, the influence of number sense on early math development and more complex mathematical thinking carries implications for instruction.'

They describe number sense as 'an emerging construct (Berch 1998) that refers to a child's fluidity and flexibility with numbers, the sense of what numbers mean and an ability to perform mental mathematics and to look at the world and make comparisons' (Gersten and Chard 1999). Parrish, drawing on Fosnot and Dolk (2001), defines fluency as 'knowing how a number can be composed and decomposed and using that information to be flexible and efficient with solving problems' (Parrish 2014: 159).

There is no single universally accepted definition of number sense but Back et al. (2014), through extensive research and review of case studies, identified seven common strands that go a long way to identifying exactly what is meant by number sense. These are:

1   An awareness of the relationship between number and quantity.
2   An understanding of number symbols, vocabulary, and meaning.
3   The ability to engage in systematic counting, including notions of cardinality and ordinality.
4   An awareness of magnitude and comparisons between different magnitudes.
5   An understanding of different representations of number.
6   Competence with simple mathematical operations.
7   An awareness of number patterns, including recognizing missing numbers.

Sood and Jitendra note that 'Number sense develops gradually over time as a result of exploring numbers, visualising them in a variety of contexts, and relating them in ways that are not limited by traditional algorithms' (2007: 146). This extract emphasizes the flexibility with number that epitomizes number sense. Number sense is the ability to be flexible with numbers and to understand both how our number system works and how numbers relate to each other. Children with good number sense have a range of mathematical strategies at their disposal and they know when to use them and how to adapt them to meet different situations.

What does good number sense look like?

Children with good number sense will be able to manipulate numbers to make calculations easier and will be flexible in their approach to solving problems. They will have good intuition for the reasonableness of an answer, and will routinely estimate answers before calculating. They look for connections and will readily spot patterns in number, using this to help them to predict future outcomes. These children have at their disposal a range of approaches to calculating and problem-solving and are able to to adapt them as needed. Children with good number sense enjoy playing with and exploring numbers and number relationships. These children are, in essence, doing an easier version of maths and they are able to find the quickest, most efficient route to the solution.

What does poor number sense look like?

Children with poor number sense will be very procedure focused and will tend to rely on a few methods that they feel secure with. They will apply inefficient and immature strategies to calculations and will fail to spot links and connections that could get them to the answer more quickly. They prefer using pen and paper rather than working things out in their heads. They are reluctant to estimate an answer before working it out and will generally accept whatever answer they arrive at, without considering whether it is reasonable or not. This was well illustrated to me by a Year 5 child who was tackling a question that required her to estimate the sum of two 4-digit numbers before calculating the answer. She approached this task by calculating the answer and then giving an estimate. I asked her why she was doing it that way around and she replied: 'It is much easier to find an estimate for the answer after you have worked out what the answer is.' You have to admire her logic – if nothing else!

Children with poor number sense do not enjoy maths and won't spend time playing around with and exploring numbers. These children do a harder version of maths that relies upon remembering and applying procedures, with little understanding of the underlying numerical concepts. By developing number sense, we can help children who are struggling to access the 'easier' version of maths and to develop strategies to simplify calculations.

Strategies to develop number sense

Number sense can be developed over time by providing opportunities to explore and play with numbers, to visualize numbers in different contexts, and to spot and predict the patterns and relationships between numbers. Burns (2007) highlighted the following key research-based strategies to help develop number sense.

Explore and evaluate different methods for computing

Provide problems that have multiple solutions and encourage the children to think of different ways to solve a problem. This helps them to move away from the idea that there is one way and one way only of solving a problem and will encourage them to reason mathematically. It also exposes them to ideas and strategies that they may not have previously considered. If children have only been shown one method, then their focus will be on remembering and using that method rather than thinking about what the numbers mean and how they work together.

For example, consider this apparently straightforward question from Mike Askew's blog [http://mikeaskew.net/page7/files/Creativity.html]:

> Which number is the odd one out?
>
> 15   20   23   25
>
> 20? The only even number
> 15? The only number that is not in the 20s
> 23? The only prime number
> 25? The only square number

There are several reasons why each of these numbers could be the odd one out and this type of activity will help to develop number sense, particularly if all the reasons that the children come up with are shared and evaluated. It is also a very inclusive problem, as every child will be able to come up with one number that they think is the odd one out and why. The mathematical richness in this activity comes with the discussions and reasons why each number could be the odd one out.

Work in groups to discuss strategies for calculation

Vygotsky's (1978) constructivist view of learning explained that children construct their understanding through social interaction. It is through discussing ideas with their peers, using language that comes naturally to them, that they build their understanding of mathematical concepts. This is most effective when accompanied by appropriate questioning from the teacher, to make sure that the discussions are of a high quality and that they are deepening the children's understanding of the mathematical concepts.

Encourage children to calculate mentally

This is something that children with poor number sense will be loath to do, but it takes them out of their comfort zone and makes them look for easier ways of working something out. For example, if they are asked to add up 4 + 7 + 6 + 3, they will be more inclined to look for the connections (in this case bonds to ten) if they have to do it mentally rather than using pen and paper, or concrete materials. Encouraging children to work calculations out using mental strategies moves them away from using written methods and will help to develop number sense rather than a reliance on rote learning and procedure.

Encourage the children to estimate in real life contexts

Children with poor number sense don't estimate – they don't see the point in doing more work than they have already been set. However, if we can show them the relevance of estimation and how it can make life easier for them, then they will be more likely to do it. For example:

> Roughly how many children are in the playground? If we have 200 cartons of milk, will that be enough? How many more might we need?

> Roughly how many weeks will it take to save £100 if I get £9 pocket money a week?

Question children about their reasoning

The 'are you sure?' question is generally used when a child has made a mistake, but it can be a much more powerful question if used when they have got the answer right. Asking this question makes the learner defend their thinking and verbalize their reasoning. Many children who would be considered more able find this quite challenging, as they 'just know' the answer. However, for the less able child this opportunity to explain their reasoning can really help them to develop and crystallize their thinking.

Provide the maths context

All too often children are presented with lists of calculations, with no context at all. For example, 362 + 143. Without a reason to make the calculation, many children will consider it irrelevant. Encourage the children to think what this problem could apply to. What could we have 362 of? What could we have 143 of? Why might we need to add these two numbers together?

Explore the suggestions that they come up with. Are they realistic? Can we estimate the answer first? How might we do that? How accurate do we need to be? Does that accuracy depend on the context?

Developing number sense

A great example of how to develop number sense comes from Jo Boaler's book *Mathematical Mindsets* (2016). In this example she asked a group of employees from a company specializing in developing online courses to find a solution for 18 × 5. They did this with ease, and after discussing the similarities and differences between their approaches, Jo started to draw visual representations of their solutions, as shown in Figure 7.1.

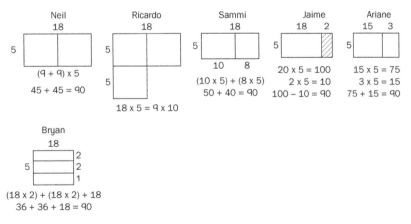

Figure 7.1 Visual representation of different approaches

It was at this point that the employees started to get really excited, as they had not previously considered how many different ways there were to approaching such an apparently straightforward problem. They were also amazed how the visual representations of their solutions showed the underlying mathematical principles so clearly.

Thus demonstrating that there are many ways to represent a solution, all of which are mathematically correct.

Making connections

Maths is a very interconnected subject, yet it is often taught in a very disconnected way. Some children will work out these connections given time, but for children with a specific learning difficulty in maths, these links and connections will need to be explicitly pointed out.

One way of doing this is to use a triangle formation (trios) to show the connection between addition and subtraction and also for the connection between multiplication and division. For example, taking the numbers 4, 5, and 9 we can show how these are linked using the diagram in Figure 7.2. Similarly, we can show the relationship between 2, 5, and 10 using the diagram in Figure 7.3.

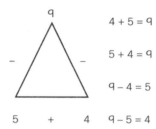

$$4 + 5 = 9$$
$$5 + 4 = 9$$
$$9 - 4 = 5$$
$$9 - 5 = 4$$

Figure 7.2 Trio for the numbers 4, 5, and 9

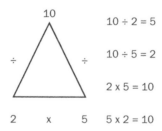

$$10 \div 2 = 5$$
$$10 \div 5 = 2$$
$$2 \times 5 = 10$$
$$5 \times 2 = 10$$

Figure 7.3 Trio for the numbers 2, 5, and 10

Area and multiplication

Linking area and multiplication can really help a learner to understand written methods (e.g. the grid method) and to help them to 'see' the concept of multiplication.

Consider the calculation 16×14. We can relate this to the area of a rectangle that is 16 cm by 14 cm, as illustrated in Figure 7.4.

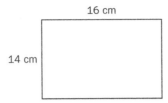

Figure 7.4 Calculating 16 × 14

Now, imagine a 10 cm by 10 cm square hiding inside the rectangle as depicted in Figure 7.5. If we now divide the rectangle up into four parts we can represent it as in Figure 7.6. This links easily now to the grid method as in Figure 7.7.

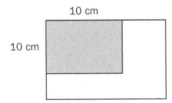

Figure 7.5 A 10 cm × 10 cm square inside a rectangle

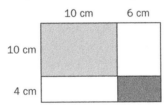

Figure 7.6 Rectangle divided up into four parts

X	10	6
10	100	60
4	40	24

Figure 7.7 The grid method

$(x + 6) (x + 4) = x^2 + 6x + 4x + 24$

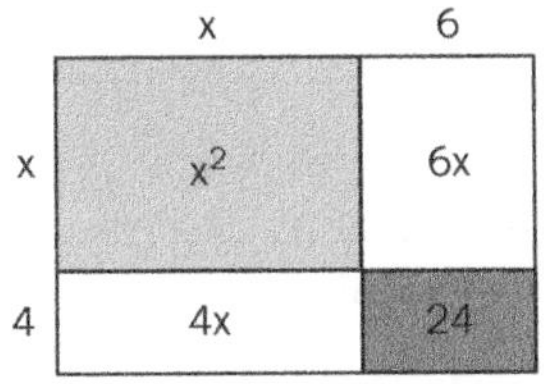

	x	6
x	x^2	6x
4	4x	24

Figure 7.8 Multiplying out brackets in quadratic equations

We can even extend this thinking to link to how we multiply out brackets in quadratic equations, as shown in Figure 7.8.

Number talks

Number talks are another very effective way of developing number sense. They help children to make sense of mathematics, to develop efficient computation strategies, and to develop communication and reasoning. They also are a great way to encourage children to make checking and proving their solutions a routine part of their approach to maths.

There are five essential components to a number talk.

The environment

For number talks to be successful, all participants need to feel safe and secure, so that they can openly express and explore their ideas without fear of ridicule. One way to ensure this is to foster a culture where mistakes are accepted, and any one idea is valued as much as any other, whether it is right, wrong or even totally implausible. The teacher's role is to accept and explore all the solutions offered without giving any feedback as to whether they are correct or not. Then each idea is taken in turn, explored and discussed, and the children are given the opportunity to defend and explain their thinking. One of the main causes of maths anxiety is the fear of getting the answer wrong and looking 'stupid' in front of your peers, and number talks can go a long way to dispelling such fear.

Class talk

Once the teacher has presented the number problem, the children then have the opportunity to discuss it and to come up with their solutions and strategies. They can show the teacher that they have come up with a solution by raising a thumb. If they have more than one solution, they can raise more fingers. The teacher will then ask the children to give their solutions and each one will be recorded on the white board for the class to discuss.

Spending time on one problem in this way and exploring all ideas and solutions helps the children to clarify their understanding of the concept (Piaget 1936) and it also helps to iron out any misconceptions that they may have had. It also helps the children to develop fluency and flexibility in maths, as they are being exposed to different ideas and different ways of solving a problem. Another advantage is that it helps children to test out their theories and to decide which strategy is the most efficient.

Teacher's role

The teacher's role here is to facilitate rather than to tell. It is a case of teaching less and listening more (Piaget 1936) and questioning the children to help draw out their ideas and understanding. The idea is for the teacher to guide the discussion, to help the children to see connections and relationships between different solutions and to explore the reasons why some solutions don't work. The ownership of the learning is very much with the children, and the teacher is the guide.

Mental maths

Mental maths is an integral part of number talks. Encouraging learners to work out solutions mentally stops them relying on procedures and standard algorithms. When you work something out mentally you are much more likely to be flexible with the numbers and to consider how they relate to each other, as you are looking for the quickest and most efficient route to the answer. If you are given paper and pencil you are more likely to apply the method without really thinking about the value of the numbers. For example, if you were adding 99 and 49 mentally, you are much more likely to think of it as 100 plus 50 and then take away 2. If you have a paper and pencil, you may just revert to column addition, which is not helping to develop number sense at all.

Choice of problem

It is important that the number talks will enable the children to explore multiple solutions. Ideally, they should encourage the children to see the relationships between numbers and to look for patterns. The number talk problem should be accessible for all learners, but at the same time allow children to add depth to their understanding.

For an example of number talk, see Box 7.1.

Box 7.1: Example of number talk	
How would you solve 9 × 16 mentally?	
Method 1: Break a factor into smaller factors 9 × 16 = 9 × (8 × 2) = 72 × 2 = 144	**Method 2: Use partial products** 9 × 10 = 90 9 × 6 = 54 90 + 54 = 144
Method 3: Use numbers that are easier to work with 9 × 16 Use 10 × 16 instead 10 × 16 = 160 Subtract 1 × 16 160 − 16 = 144	**Method 4: Use doubling and halving** 9 × 16 18 × 8 36 × 4 72 × 2 144 × 1= 144

DYSLEXIA: STRATEGIES TO IMPROVE MEMORY

There are many strategies that we can use to support a poor memory. Before we look at those, however, it is important to consider what sort of information we are more likely to remember and what sort of information we are likely to forget.

What we remember most

Information presented at the beginning and at the end of a lesson or talk

This phenomenon is called the primacy/recency effect (Sousa 2012). The *primacy* effect entails that we find it much easier to remember information that is given at the beginning of a learning session, whereas the *recency* effect entails that we also find it easier to remember information that is given at the end. The period in the middle of a learning session is referred to as 'downtime'. So, the beginning and end of a learning session are prime-time windows for learning. The first part of the session should be for new learning, the middle part – the downtime – for review and consolidation, and the final part for processing the information and assigning meaning to it, helping us to understand it and store it in our long-term memory. To maximize the effect, the learning sessions should be relatively short, say around 20–25 minutes.

Information associated with other information

We are much more likely to remember something if we can link it to something that we already know. In terms of maths, we need to encourage children to link the new learning to a mathematical concept or fact that they already know. Maths is a highly interconnected discipline and the more we can appreciate and capitalize on these connections the better (Sharma 2008).

Extraordinary things

Anything that is out of the ordinary is easier to remember. If we have had a period of time at work, say, when one day is pretty much the same as another, it can be hard to recall when or where a particular event happened, because there is so much similarity between the days. But then, something extraordinary happens, such as the fire alarm going off and everyone has to evacuate the building. It is much more likely that you will be able to recall the day that that happened for a long time after the event, as it is so extraordinary.

So, for maths learning, we need to try and turn the mundane into the extraordinary. Imagery and visualization can help here. Instead of using pizzas and cakes for fraction work, why not illustrate the fractions with something more unusual, such as a circular multi-coloured alien planet.

Repeated information

Overlearning is a key strategy in supporting memory. Information that we only receive once will be poorly registered in the brain and will soon be forgotten. However, the more times we revisit that piece of information, the more we are likely to remember it. A good analogy for this is to compare the way that we learn something to walking through a field of tall grass. As we walk through the grass, a pathway will be formed where we have trodden on the grass. The next morning, the grass will have bounced back and the pathway that we made will have disappeared. If we walk along that same pathway, every day for 2 or 3 weeks, then the grass won't recover and a permanent pathway will become visible. Our memory works in the same way: we have to keep retracing our steps to make a permanent neural pathway.

Information that links to us personally

We are much more likely to remember something if we are interested in it, and most people find themselves pretty interesting! So, we need to try and relate new learning to something that links to the child personally. If, for instance, they are very interested in dinosaurs or football, we can reword maths problems so that they relate to the child's interests.

Information that evokes social/emotional experiences

The stronger the emotions triggered by new information, the more likely we are to remember it. This could be any type of emotional reaction, negative or positive. We also remember information that we have learned in a social context more than in isolation, which is why cooperative learning can be such a powerful memory enhancer (Vygotsky 1978). Ericksen (1984: 51) summarized this well when he said: 'Students learn what they care about and remember what they understand.'

The 4 Ms

We can divide strategies to support memory into four categories. The strategies depend on making the information:

1   Manageable
2   Multisensory
3   Memorable
4   Meaningful.

Make it manageable

Memory problems often occur because the working memory has been overloaded. This can be alleviated by:

Providing time to access working memory

Make sure that time is given to process new information and to access working memory – this can take as long as 8 seconds. The time that a teacher waits for a learner to provide an answer is known as 'wait time'. Tobin (1986) found that most teachers were only giving children between 1 and 2 seconds to respond. This is nowhere near the 8 seconds that some learners with poor working memory need. And when studying the optimum wait time in maths, Lerman (2014) showed that performance improves with increased wait time.

Teaching the child how to discard irrelevant information

This is especially the case in word problems. Children often become bogged down by the detail in a word problem, most of which has no bearing on the maths.

For example, consider the following word problem.

> Sarah, Amir, and Joanna all enjoyed collecting football cards, for their favourite team, Manchester United. They had 60 cards altogether. If they shared them out equally, how many would they each have.

Most of the words in this problem are totally irrelevant, but some children 'can't see the wood for the tress' and need to be taught how to extract the relevant information.

One popular method is the RUCSAC method: Read, Underline, Calculate, Solve, Answer, Check. However, this method should be used with caution, as it is really another example of emphasizing process over understanding. Many word problems contain ambiguous language. For example, consider the following two questions:

> How many more than 23 is 27?
> This requires the calculation $27 - 23 = 4$

> What is 4 more than 23?
> This requires the calculation $23 + 4 = 27$

The language is very similar in both cases, but the calculations required are different.

The best way to help children with word problems is to develop their understanding of the bar model method (see page 176), which will help them to see the deeper structures in the problem and to construct a model of the problem that will show them what calculations are required.

Encouraging the child to look for patterns and connections

The more we do this in maths, the less the load on working memory. Children who cannot make connections or see patterns face a huge task, as they have to remember each piece of information as novel and discrete from anything else. If they can find patterns and connections they will have less to remember, helping them to assimilate new facts and make new connections.

Working for short periods

As we have seen from the primacy/recency effect, it is better to work for small periods of time and to take frequent breaks. These breaks do not need to be very long, just a few seconds will do. So asking the learner to fetch a book from the shelf or to have a glass of water may be all that is required.

Making a set of memory cards

One strategy that I find very helpful is to make a set of memory cards. These are credit-card-sized blank cards that can be used to note down anything that the learner is finding hard to remember. It may be something like a times table fact, a calculation procedure or some mathematical vocabulary. The cards are then practised on a daily basis, and this 'overlearning' though frequent practice is a great way to get the information into the long-term memory.

Writing out the times table square

With practice most learners can master this quite quickly and should aim to be able to write out the complete times table square in less than 5 minutes. The first thing to do is draw the grid, either 10 × 10 or 12 × 12. Then fill in the 'easy' parts; for example, the 1× table, followed by the 2×, 5×, and 10× tables. Make sure that the learner understands that 2 × 5 has the same product as 5 × 2 (the commutative property of multiplication, so for each times table they will complete a row and the corresponding column).

The learner can then choose which table to complete next. They might choose the 9× because it has such a distinct pattern, or maybe the 4 because it is double 2×. Carry on in this way and the learner will soon see that there are only a few facts left to fill in and these can be derived from other facts if the learner can't remember them (see Box 7.2).

Box 7.2: Example times table square

×	1	2	3	4	5	6	7	8	9	10
1	1	2	3	4	5	6	7	8	9	10
2	2	4	6	8	10	12	14	16	18	20
3	3	6		12	15				27	30
4	4	8	12	16	20	24	28	32	36	40
5	5	10	15	20	25	30	35	40	45	50
6	6	12		24	30				54	60
7	7	14		28	35				63	70
8	8	16		32	40				72	80
9	9	18	27	36	45	54	63	72	81	90
10	10	20	30	40	50	60	70	80	90	100

Learning to use a calculator

This may sound pretty obvious, but many learners don't know how to use a calculator properly and often believe any answer that it provides. A calculator app, the 'Dyscalculator', has now been developed specifically for dyscalculic learners. The app includes options to help learners who have trouble identifying numbers, finding the difference between numbers, ordering numbers or deciding which operations to use. Numbers are displayed in symbolic, written, and audio format. It is free to download and appropriate for learners age 6 upwards.

Make it multisensory

Information is received into the brain through our senses: sight, sound, touch, smell, and taste. In terms of learning, children tend to have a preferred learning style, whereby they respond better to information that is presented aurally, visually or kinaesthetically. Many children with a specific learning difficulty have a weakness in one or more of these channels. Teaching in a multisensory way, using all three channels simultaneously, will help children, as their stronger channels will support their weaker ones. It won't be of benefit to the child simply to present the information in their preferred format, as this won't help strengthen the weaker channels. Also, the more ways that information is presented, the more likely we are to remember it. This is because the information will have been registered in multiple ways. If you only receive information via one channel, then you only have one route to retrieving that information.

The following well-known saying summarizes the benefit of multi-sensory teaching:

> We remember 10% of what we hear
> We remember 30% of what we hear and see
> We remember 40% of what we hear, see, and say
> We remember 70–100% of what we hear, see, say, and do

Visual strategies

We can make information that is presented visually more memorable by using colour to highlight key chunks or enlarging key numbers and operations so that they stand out. Mind maps can be used to help see the connections in maths, as shown in Figure 7.9. This particular mind map was created using the kidspiration mind mapping tool available at: www.inspiration.com.

Visualizing the problem can support a weak verbal memory and can also develop links with the visuospatial memory. Drawing out the mathematical model can really help with conceptual understanding. The ultimate goal here is that the child will eventually be able to visualize the model in their mind's eye without having to draw it. Children find it hard to draw the maths, so this will require practice. Take, for example, the following word problem:

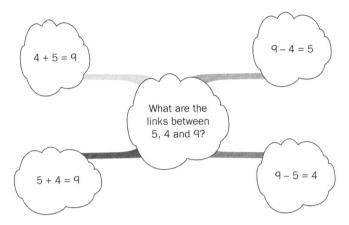

Figure 7.9 Mind map

Sam has saved up some money. His father gives him twice the amount that he has saved.

When he goes shopping, Sam spends £45 on a pair of trainers, and a third of the remaining money on a book that costs £15.

What had Sam saved originally?

This seems like quite a tricky word problem, but it can be greatly simplified by drawing out a mathematical model. The amounts involved could be depicted as follows:

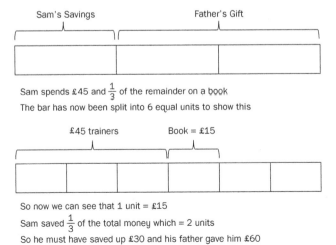

After buying the trainers for £45, one-third of Sam's remaining money is spent on a book, so the final section of the diagram can be split into thirds, with each section being worth £15.

We can see from the diagram that Sam had £90 in total, so he must have saved up £30 (and his father gave him 2 × £30 = £60).

Auditory strategies: mnemonics

Mnemonics are memory devices that help learners recall pieces of information. For example, 'Cherry Pie is delicious' is a mnemonic that can help with recall of the formula for the circumference of a circle:

$$C = \pi D$$

This can then be followed by 'Apple pies are 2', which can be used to help recall of the formula for the area of a circle:

$$A = \pi r^2$$

It is a good idea to use mnemonics sparingly, as if you use too many, you will end up needing a mnemonic to remember all your mnemonics!

Verbal strategies

Verbalizing mathematical diagrams. Mathematical diagrams can be more deeply understood if they are verbalized through elaboration. Describing and discussing a mathematical diagram can really help a learner to understand the maths involved. This is very well illustrated by Patricia Babtie, a dyscalculia specialist at Emerson House in London (see Figure 7.10).

In this activity the learner had been asked to copy the pattern shown by the blocks. Their first attempt was quite poor and not a very accurate reproduction of the pattern. The second attempt was a vast improvement and was achieved after just 30 minutes of talking. The learner had been given the opportunity to describe the shapes in each square, using directional language and talking about how the triangles related to each other. What a difference, and all achieved through verbalizing their perception of a visual image.

VISUAL PERCEPTION
Drawing triangles from a pattern of cubes

Diagram of pattern to be copied

Copy pattern using Mozi blocks

Draw diagram from block pattern
First attempt

Second attempt 30 minutes later

Pupil describes the shapes in each square before drawing, including using directional language to explain where the corners of the triangle are in relation to the square.

VISUAL PERCEPTION

Figure 7.10 Describing and discussing a mathematical diagram

Verbal rehearsal. Verbal rehearsal involves repeating the information over and over again. It is a strategy that most of us use if we are trying to remember a telephone number or a car registration. It can be a very effective way of transferring mathematical facts from short-term to long-term memory.

Kinaesthetic strategies

Children need to be engaged in feeling and touching as much as possible. Thus the use of concrete materials is imperative if we want them to have the best chance of success. Even if concrete materials are not available, children should be encouraged to visualize them or imagine that they are using them. (Chapter 9 explores the use of concrete materials further.)

Make it memorable

For information to stay in the memory, it must be clearly and firmly registered. Registration needs to be:

- *Clear and unambiguous*. Long, multi-step instructions should be broken down into smaller steps that will be easier to remember.
- *Rehearsed and reinforced*. The learner should be encouraged to repeat and rehearse the information on a daily basis to make the most of 'overlearning'.
- *Understood and connected to existing information*. Help the learner to connect the new information to something that they already know.
- *Actively attended to*. Make sure that the learner is not only listening, but is also actively trying to understand and remember.

Transferring from the left to the right side of the brain

Another strategy that will help us to remember information is to transfer it from one side of the brain to the other. One of the most inefficient ways of learning something is to read it and copy it out, yet this is the approach that many learners take when they are revising for exams. A much more effective way of revising is to do something with the information and to transform it in some way. If we just read and copy or read and summarize, then all the effort is located in the left-hand side of the brain. However, if we can move the information to the right-hand side of the brain, this will make it much more memorable. This could be in the form of drawing a mind map, acting something out, creating a picture, explaining it to someone else, or making up a song. There are many ways that we can transfer information from the left-hand side of the brain to the right – we just need to think creatively and visually.

Make it meaningful

We are much more likely to remember information that relates to us personally in some way. So when we are working on a mathematical concept, it can be of benefit to relate it to real-life experiences. Underpinning concepts with mathematical models, either in diagrams or using concrete materials, will help to add meaning.

For example, children with maths difficulties often find it hard to recall number bonds to ten.

$$1 + 9 = 10$$
$$2 + 8 = 10$$
$$3 + 7 = 10, \text{ etc.}$$

These number bonds can seem like a series of unrelated facts that just have to be learned. However, if the bonds are represented in a tens frame, then the reason why they are paired this way becomes apparent and the child will have a strong visual image of why 3 and 7 go together to make 10. Whenever you see three filled spaces in the ten frame, there will be seven empty spaces and vice versa, as in Figure 7.11.

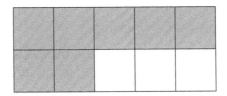

Figure 7.11 Three unfilled spaces in the ten frame

The child can then be encouraged to think of a real-life situation in which we would need to know that 3 and 7 make 10. For example, I have saved up £3 and I was given £7 for my birthday. How much money do I have altogether?

Directed discovery

Another strategy to help make memories more meaningful is to use directed discovery. We are much more likely to remember something if we have discovered it for ourselves. There is a tendency in maths teaching to take the stance that all the maths in the world has been discovered and it is the teacher's job to tell the students all about it.

This takes the curiosity and sense of exploration out of maths. So, for example, instead of saying to the child, 'today we are going to look at doubles and near doubles', give them the opportunity to discover these relationships for themselves.

One way that this could be achieved is by using a standard set of dominoes. Start off by playing a normal game of dominoes and then ask the child if they have noticed anything special about some of the dominoes. Some of them have the same number of dots on both sides. Discussion can follow about the other dominoes and whether any are closely related to the double ones. In this way the child has a vested interest in the new learning, as they have discovered it for themselves and feel some ownership in the new idea.

Categorize and make connections

Some children with maths difficulties find this very hard to do. The connections are not obvious to them and need to be explicitly pointed out. By showing them how new learning can link to prior learning, we can help them to make sense of what they are being taught and they will be much more likely to remember it.

Activities to support working memory

Digit span recall. A sequence of numbers is given to the learner. This can be done either visually or orally. If the digits are to be given visually, they can be written on a card or presented with wooden or plastic numbers. The child then looks at the card for 5 seconds before it is removed. If the digits are presented orally, they should be delivered in a monotone voice, one second apart. The child then has to recall the digits in the correct sequence.

This activity can be made more challenging, by:

- increasing the number of items in the sequence;
- increasing the time delay between presentation and response;
- introducing an element of distraction, such as asking the child to recall something that they did at the weekend, or getting them to collect something from another classroom;
- asking for the sequence to be recalled in reverse order.

Kim's game. A selection of items is placed on a tray and the child is given 10 seconds to try to remember all of the items on the tray.

This game can be made more challenging by increasing the number of items on the tray, by decreasing the time given to look at them, and by adding an element of distraction before recall. Strategies to improve recall should be highlighted for the child, such as verbal rehearsal or connecting all the items on the tray with a story.

Ten frame flash. In this game, a ten frame is presented to the child with a number of counters or cubes placed on the frame, as shown in Figure 7.12. The child has 5 seconds to look at the position of the counters on the frame and is then given a blank ten frame and a box of counters so that they can replicate the arrangement of counters. This game can be varied by changing the number of counters, the complexity of the arrangement, the time given to remember the arrangement, and by using delay or distraction between memorizing and recall.

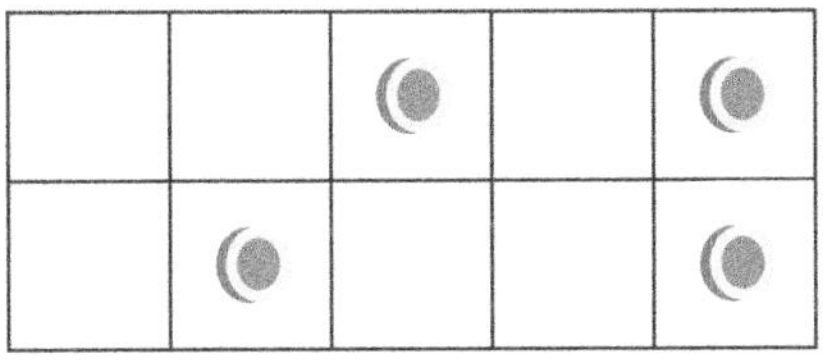

Figure 7.12 Counters on a ten frame

This game can also be played aurally. In this case, the child will have a set of counters and a blank ten frame and they will then listen to your instructions, as you describe the position of each counter. This is a great way to help them to use and understand mathematical language as well as improving their memory function.

Shopping game. This is a well-known parlour game in which each player adds something to the list of items being bought. For example, the first player may say: 'I went shopping and I bought a banana.' The second player has then to recall the item that has been bought and add their own: 'I went shopping and I bought a banana and a jacket.' Play continues until someone makes a mistake.

There are many variations of this game, including:

'I went on holiday and I packed . . .'
'I went to the zoo and I saw . . .'

The more unrelated the items are, the harder the game will be.

Card games. Games such as Crazy eights, Pelmanism, and Go fish rely on memory and practise mathematical concepts. This can be a fun way to develop memory strategies.

1   *Crazy eights.* For this game you will need a standard pack of cards. Each player is dealt five cards and the remaining cards are placed face down on the table. The top card is turned over for play to commence. Each player must either play a card or pick from the 'draw' pile. Cards can be played in the following way:

   • If the top card of the discard pile is not an eight, you may play any card which matches the rank or suit of the previous card (for example, if the top card was the King of hearts you could play any king or any heart).
   • An eight may be played on any card, and the player of the eight must nominate a suit.
   • If an eight is on top of the pile, you must play either another eight or any card of the suit nominated by the person who played the eight.
   • The first player to discard all of their cards is the winner.

2   *Pelmanism.* There are endless versions of this game. Remove all the picture cards from the pack and place the remaining cards face down on the table. They are usually arranged in rows and columns. A player selects two cards. If they are a matching pair, they keep the cards and have another go. If the two cards do not match, they are replaced in the correct position and play passes to the next player. The player with the most pairs is the winner. Here are a just a few ideas for different version of the game:

   • *Number match*: A pair of cards match if they have the same number.
   • *Odd or even match.* The cards match if they are both odd or are both even.
   • *Addition match.* The cards match if they add up to a particular total – for example, 12. The cards used will need to be carefully selected so that there are sufficient pairs that add up to 12 and that all the cards will be used.

- *Multiplication match.* The cards match if they multiply to a certain number. Again, the set of cards used will need to be carefully selected.
- *Fraction/decimal/percentage match.* For this game you will need to make your own set of cards, showing fractions, decimals, and percentages. The cards will match if they show the equivalent numerical amount. For example, 1/2 would match with 0.5.

3   *Go fish.* Each player is dealt seven cards and the remaining cards are spread out face down on the table. This is called the pool. The aim of the game it to collect sets of four cards all with the same face value, say four aces. Players ask each other for particular cards that will help them to make a set of four. Any sets of four that are made will be placed on the table. If the person does not have that particular card, they will say 'Go fish' and take a card from the pool. Play continues until all the cards have been placed in sets of four on the table. The person with the most sets of four is the winner.

DYSPRAXIA: STRATEGIES TO IMPROVE VISUAL SPATIAL AWARENESS

Classroom strategies

Verbalization

Dyspraxic children will often become confused when given information visually and verbally at the same time. They will tend to completely ignore the visual information. We can support this by giving them the visual information separately from the verbal information and also by making sure that the verbal information is clear and has been registered by the child. Concrete materials will be useful here to support the verbal information and add a tangible visual element.

Seating

Make sure that the dyspraxic learner is seated with clear line of sight of the teacher. If they are easily distracted by light, ensure they are seated somewhere quiet (i.e. not by the classroom door) and that they are not sat directly under strip lighting.

Presentation of information

Provide handouts in advance that are clear and uncluttered, and they should be double-spaced. Try to avoid any need to copy information from the board or give extra time for copying if it is unavoidable. Scaffold examples of how to set out maths problems and provide templates of these for the child to refer back to.

Resources

Aperture cards can be very helpful for a learner faced with a page of calculations. Make the aperture by cutting a small window out of a piece of card. The card is then placed over the page of calculations so that only one calculation is visible. Reading rules and coloured overlays can also be used.

L-shaped cards can help a dyspraxic learner to read information from a graph or table. Writing slopes are also widely available. The learner may also benefit from specialized pens and pencils, or pencil grips as well as grip rulers to help them when they are drawing graphs or constructing geometric figures.

Numicon

Numicon (see Figure 7.13) is a very popular maths resource and one that has been found to be particularly helpful with dyspraxic children (see: www.numicon.com).

Figure 7.13 Numicon

Activities to develop visuospatial awareness

Simon says

This can be a great way of developing listening skills and coordination in dyspraxic learners. The number of instructions can be increased as appropriate.

Obstacle course

Create an obstacle course in the hall or playground. Let the learner follow the course two or three times and then ask them to recall the layout by either describing the course or drawing it.

Barrier games

For this game you will need to draw a simple picture and then sit opposite the child with a barrier between you, so that they can't see the picture. Describe to them how to draw your picture in as much detail as you can. Then you can swap over so that the child describes a picture that they have drawn for you to replicate.

References

Back, J., Sayers, J. and Andrews, P. (2014) The development of foundational number sense in England and Hungary: a case study comparison, in B. Ubuz, Ç. Haser and M.A. Mariotti (eds.) *Proceedings of the Eighth Conference of the European Society for Research in Mathematics Education* (pp. 1835–44). Antalya: ERME.

Berch, D.B. (1998) Mathematical cognition: from numerical thinking to mathematics education. Paper presented at the National Institute of Child Health and Human Development Conference, Bethesda, MD, April.

Boaler, J. (2016) *Mathematical Mindsets: Unleashing students' potential through creative math*. New York: Wiley.

Burns, M. (2007) *About Teaching Mathematics: A K-8 resource* (3rd edn.). Sausalito, CA: Math Solutions Publications.

Ericksen, S. (1984) *The Essence of Good Teaching: Helping students learn and remember what they learn*. San Francisco, CA: Jossey-Bass.

Fosnot, C.T. and Dolk, M. (2001) *Young Mathematicians at Work: Constructing number sense, addition, and subtraction*. Portsmouth, NH: Heinemann.

Gersten, R. and Chard, D. (1999) Number sense: rethinking arithmetic instruction for students with mathematical disabilities, *Journal of Special Education*, 33(1): 18–28 [www.ldonline.org/article/5838; accessed 22 May 2017].

Lerman, S. (2014) *Encyclopaedia of Mathematics Education*. Dordrecht: Springer.

Parrish, S. (2014) *Number Talks: Whole number computation, Grades K-5: A multimedia professional learning resource*. Sausalito, CA: Math Solutions Publications.

Piaget, J. (1936) *Origins of Iintelligence in the Child*. London: Routledge & Kegan Paul.

Sharma, M.C. (2008) *Dyslexia, Dyscalculia, and other Mathematics Language Difficulties*. Framingham, MA: CT/LM.

Sood, S. and Jitendra, A.K. (2007) A comparative analysis of number sense instruction in reform-based and traditional mathematics textbooks, *Journal of Special Education*, 41(3): 145–57.

Sousa, D.A. (2012) *The Primacy-Recency Effect* [retrieved from: www.brainbasedee.wordpress.com/2012/10/12/the-Primacy-Recency-effect/; accessed 15 September 2016].

Tobin, K. (1986) Effects of teacher wait time on discourse characteristics in mathematics and language arts classes, *American Educational Research Journal*, 23(2): 191–200.

Vygotsky, L. (1978) *Mind in Society: The development of higher psychological processes*. Cambridge, MA: Harvard University Press.

Characteristics

The essence of mathematics is not to make simple things complicated, but to make complicated things simple.

Stan Gudder (1993)

This chapter looks at the characteristics of *mathematics* and the characteristics of *mathematicians*.

Understanding the characteristics of maths

The concrete, pictorial, abstract approach

One of the most useful approaches when supporting a learner with maths difficulties is the concrete, pictorial, abstract approach (CPA). This perspective on early learning in maths is attributed to Jerome Bruner in the 1960s. His theory was that to really understand a mathematical concept we need to experience it in three different ways. These stages of understanding are the enactive, the iconic, and the symbolic.

Enactive/concrete stage

In the first stage, the learner uses concrete materials, such as cubes, counters, Cuisenaire rods or base ten materials, to model and explore the mathematical concept. Thinking and understanding is through physical actions and concrete representations. The mathematical idea is 'acted out' with real objects and this provides the foundation for conceptual understanding. For example, multi-link cubes might be used to represent twelve divided by two, as shown in Figure 8.1.

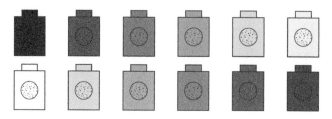

Figure 8.1 Division represented by multi-link cubes

Iconic/pictorial stage

The second stage is the iconic or pictorial stage. This stage relates the 'hands-on' concrete experience to pictorial representations, such as a diagram or picture of the problem. So twelve divided by two might be shown as in Figure 8.2. This stage helps children to visualize the concept when they don't have the concrete materials in front of them.

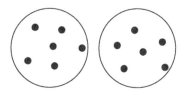

Figure 8.2 Division depicted pictorially

Symbolic/abstract stage

The third stage is the symbolic or abstract stage. Here, mathematical symbols and notations are used to represent the mathematical concept. At this stage, twelve divided by two would be represented as:

$$12 \div 2 = 6$$

Bruner (1960) also described a spiral curriculum, where topics in maths are revisited, each time with greater depth and complexity. He believed this to be the most effective way of helping children to gain mastery in the subject. This would be good practice for any teacher but is particularly important for learners with specific difficulties in maths who require time to consolidate and accommodate new information.

Sharma (1986) built on Bruner's CPA theory. Sharma believes that to fully understand a mathematical concept, it should be taught through six levels of knowing: intuitive, concrete, pictorial, abstract, application, and communication.

Sharma's six levels of learning a mathematical idea

Intuitive

At the intuitive level, every new fact is introduced by linking it to something the child already knows. This has two distinct advantages. First, it reduces maths anxiety and stress, as the child is presented with something that they are familiar with. Second, it makes the new learning more meaningful and more permanent, as we are much more likely to remember something new if we can link it to something we already know. Furthermore, it fosters the idea that one mathematical idea can lead to another and this will help in developing reasoning skills.

Concrete

Each new fact is presented by modelling with concrete materials. This is in line with Bruner's theory on how we acquire new knowledge. It is important that the materials are chosen to develop understanding and must be suitable for the mathematical idea that we are trying to represent. There are a variety of concrete materials that we can use, including Cuisenaire rods. Base ten materials are also commonly used and are widely available.

Being able to visualize mathematical concepts and procedures will really help learners to develop their understanding. Many children struggle with maths because they have been moved on to the abstract stage of maths too quickly, so we need to make sure that they have as much time as they need with these concrete materials.

Pictorial

The model of the new idea may be drawn or represented diagrammatically. This reinforces the ability to visualize the maths and will support the child when the concrete materials are not available. The pictorial stage acts as a bridge between the concrete and the abstract stage. It helps children to cement the visual image of the concept in their memory and will provide a further multisensory element to the lesson.

Abstract

The fourth level is where the mathematical concept can be recorded in an abstract way using mathematical symbols and numbers. This level should be explicitly linked to the concrete and pictorial stages and should then be embedded by working on application and communication. For many children, this is the end goal of a maths lesson and it leaves them at the abstract level. So maths has no real meaning to them and they can't see its application in daily life. To avoid this, Sharma introduces 'application' as the next level of learning.

Application

The fifth level is to explore the application of the new idea or concept. In this way, we show the learner the relevance of the maths that they have learned to daily life and the world around them. At this stage, the learner can be encouraged to form a number story using the new idea. This is a vital stage to develop mathematical language and to work from the abstract mathematical symbols to a 'real-life' word problem. For example, if the concept was adding 3 to 9, the application stage might be to ask under what circumstances would we need to add 3 to 9. What could we have 9 of and why would we need to add 3 more? The learner would be encouraged to come up with realistic suggestions, such as 'I have 9 toy cars and my friend has given me 3 more toy cars. How many toy cars do I have altogether?' Such scenarios don't need to be complicated, just realistic enough to illustrate the relevance of the maths to the learner.

Communications

The sixth level does not really come at the end, as it is integral to the whole process of understanding a new mathematical concept or idea. During the previous five stages, there should be plenty of dialogue between the teacher and the learner, both of whom should be answering as many questions as they are asking. For example, if the lesson is on doubling numbers, the dialogue might turn out something like this:

> *Learner*: I know that double 3 means two times 3. So double 3 is 6.
> *Teacher*: Are there any other ways that we can express double 3?
> *Learner*: We could say 3 times 2 or 2 lots of 3.
> *Teacher*: Well done. Now that we know what double 3 is, can we use that to work out other problems? Does it help us if we want to work out 3 + 4?
> *Learner*: If double 3 is 3 + 3, which equals 6, I know 3 + 4 is one more, so 3 + 4 = 7.

This stage of the process is a good opportunity to assess what the child has learned and to encourage them to generalize, reason, and extend their learning through talking and questioning.

The questioning technique

Careful questioning is an integral part of teaching a new mathematical concept. By asking the right questions, we can ascertain whether the concept has been fully understood and we can also deepen understanding and reasoning by the questions that we ask. Asking the right questions is quite a skill, and it relies on the teacher having good subject knowledge to make sure that they are asking the right type of questions.

What types of questions are best?

- open questions that demand more than a yes or no response;
- questions that will help the child to think more deeply;
- questions that will help develop metacognition.

Mathematicians are always asking themselves questions. One of the most useful questions is the 'always, sometimes, never' question. By giving the learner a statement and then asking them if it is always, sometimes or never true, you are immediately making them think more deeply. For example:

> Squares are rectangles
> Is this always, sometimes or never true?

When I add two odd numbers, I will get an even number
Is this always, sometimes or never true?

Another question that can be particularly useful is to ask whether a mathematical relationship is a coincidence or a connection. For example:

$5 \times 4 = 20$
$10 \times 2 = 20$
Is this a coincidence or is there a connection?

Questions like this will really help the learner to develop their number sense and their ability to reason and generalize.

Box 8.1: An example of questioning when problem-solving

The following questions will help to develop metacognitive awareness and will encourage the child to get into the habit of using an 'internal dialogue' of questions when they are solving problems.

● What is the problem?
● What do you know about this problem?
● What do you need to know?
● Have you solved another problem like this?
● How might you try and solve this problem?
● Are there any methods that you think will work well here?
● What is a possible solution?
● How can you check that this is a solution?

Sharma (2009) asserted that the goal of the mathematics curriculum and instruction should be to help children acquire a mathematical way of thinking so that they can recognize and appreciate the applications and beauty of mathematics. He emphasized the importance of mathematical language by identifying the need to have a 'language container for the mathematical concept'. Without this we cannot receive, comprehend or communicate a mathematical concept.

Furthermore, if this model is embedded in a culture of questioning, then the understanding can be developed to a much greater level and the fear of being wrong will disappear as the child is so used to asking questions that it becomes second nature. They begin to realize that all questions are useful and will help to further their understanding.

Sharma goes on to break down the process behind this type of Socratic questioning to illustrate its strengths and value. He explains that:

> Questions instigate language; language instigates models, models instigate thinking, thinking instigates understanding, understanding produces skills, knowledge, and mastery, mastery produces competent performance, competent performance produces long lasting self-esteem and self-esteem is the basis of motivation necessary for all learning.
>
> (Sharma 2009)

The three components of a mathematical idea

As well as the six stages of knowing, Sharma also describes the three components of a mathematical idea (Figure 8.3). These three components are:

- Language
- Concept
- Procedure.

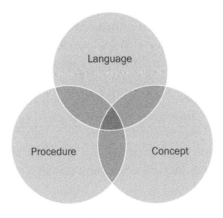

Figure 8.3 The three components of a mathematical idea

There is a tendency when teaching maths to focus on the procedure. This is particularly true leading up to maths at GCSE, as there is a great deal of pressure on teachers to make sure that all their learners achieve a pass grade in maths. For some children who may have struggled with maths throughout their schooling, there does not seem to be time to spend on making sure that the concept is understood. The focus is on being able to apply the procedure correctly. Unfortunately for these learners, if they forget the procedure, they have nothing to fall back on – in effect, they have 'nowhere to go' and will not be able to answer the question at all.

When presenting a mathematical idea, it is much more effective if equal weight is given to each of the three components:

● The language component refers to the language used in understanding, conceptualizing, and communicating mathematical information.
● The conceptual component is the mathematical idea itself.
● The procedural component is the algorithm or the method used to describe the concept.

Language

Many children struggle with understanding mathematical terminology. Terms like isosceles, denominator, and trapezium all add to the air of mystery around maths. Other terms such as product, table, and degree have multiple meanings outside the field of maths and this all adds to the confusion. For a dyslexic learner, these language difficulties can be a real barrier to achievement in maths.

One area of maths that commonly causes anxiety and confusion is the word problem. Children find it very hard to understand exactly what the problem is asking them to do. A strategy that is frequently taught is to ask the child to look for key words and key numbers. This can be a good place to start, but it is not always helpful. The following example illustrates some of the inherent difficulties.

> Jack has 3 times as much money as Sam. Together they have £120. How much money does Jack have?

From the question we can see that 3 and 120 are key numbers. A common mistake would be for the child to think that they need to divide 120 by 3. However, what we actually need to do is divide 120 by 4. But where has the 4 come from? There is no 4 in the question.

This problem can be overcome by drawing a diagram of the mathematical scenario described in the question, as demonstrated in Figure 8.4. In this case, Jack has 3 times as much money as Sam. Now it is clear that there are 4 money bags in the question and we need to divide £120 by 4 to find out how much money each bag holds. So Jack has (£120/4) × 3 = £90.

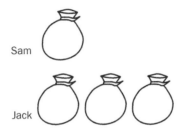

Figure 8.4 Drawing a diagram of a mathematical scenario

Another way to support learners who are struggling with the language aspect of maths is to give them practice in creating their own word problems. This is somewhat akin to learning a new language. If we only ever translate from French to English, then we are limiting our mastery of French. However, if we can translate from English to French as easily as we translate from French to English, we will become truly fluent in the language.

It is exactly the same in maths. We need to be able to 'translate' from the abstract maths to the mathematical language as well as translating from the mathematical language to the abstract maths. One way to do this is to give the children a 'number sentence' such as 5 + 4 = 9 and ask them to build a word problem around this number sentence.

Concept

The conceptual component is the mathematical idea itself. Children with difficulties in maths will need time to process the new information and will need to be given plenty of opportunities to explore it in depth, using a variety of concrete materials. They will need to 'see' the new concept modelled in multiple ways and also to see how this new concept relates to prior and future learning.

For example, let's look at the number 6. We can represent 6 in many ways:

On a number line: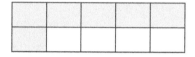

As an array:

On a ten frame:

As half of 12: $12 \div 2 = 6$

As a word: Six

As an age: Sam was 6 years old

As the number of people in a group: 'There were six children in the park':

The more ways that we can represent 6, the deeper our understanding of what 6 really is and how it relates to other numbers.

Procedure

The procedural element of the mathematical idea is the method or algorithm. For many children who struggle with maths, the procedure is all that they have. They spend their time learning rules and methods that they don't really understand and just hope that they apply them correctly. All too often, these procedures are not remembered and then the child is lost, not knowing how to attempt the question at all.

Many adults reading this will no doubt recall being taught how to divide by a fraction. The 'method' was to invert the fraction and change the divide to multiply. There was even a saying to go with this procedure:

'Ours is not to reason why, just invert and multiply!'

If ever there was a statement that summed up how not to teach maths, this must surely be it.

Principles of intervention

Fuchs et al. (2008) put forward seven principles of intervention designed to address 'serious mathematics deficits' in children aged 8–9 years. These are as follows:

1 *Instructional explicitness.* Children with specific difficulties in maths will not 'pick things up as they go along'. These children will need explicit instruction, where each step of the learning is explained and demonstrated in a clear and succinct way.
2 *Instructional design to minimize the learning challenge.* If teachers can anticipate and pre-empt the difficulty that a learner may have, then the task can be designed to minimize this difficulty. There are some concepts such as fractions and place value that are notoriously difficult and being aware of this in advance can help the teacher to tailor the task appropriately.
3 *Emphasize concept.* By providing a strong conceptual basis for the procedures that are being taught, the learner will be supported in their efforts to recall and apply the procedure. Sharma also believed that understanding of the concept should take precedence over recall of the procedure.
4 *Drill and practice.* There is a place for drill and practice because we are striving for automaticity of recall, but this is only of real value when the underlying concept has been understood. Being able to recall times tables will make life easier in maths, but it is no more a measure of mathematical ability than being able to spell being seen as a measure of being literate.
5 *Cumulative review.* This follows on from Bruner's notion of the spiral curriculum, where concepts are revisited in greater depth to ensure that they are fully understood. Cumulative review also provides the opportunity for teachers to address any areas of weakness or confusion.
6 *Motivation.* None of us wants to spend time doing something that we don't enjoy or see the point of. Motivation is key to successful learning and we need to make sure that motivation is an integral part of any maths intervention.

7   *Monitoring of ongoing progress.* This is the final and most important principle of intensive intervention. This will determine the effectiveness or otherwise of an intervention programme for a given child.

Understanding these characteristics in maths can explain why we need to focus on the concrete and pictorial elements and why we can't just teach procedure alone. The other side of the coin to this is to understand the characteristics of the mathematician.

Understanding the characteristics of mathematicians

In his article 'Generating curiosity in mathematics learning', Gilderdale (2007) examined the characteristics that good mathematicians have rather than the characteristics of the maths itself. He found that that children who were most successful in maths were the ones who could

- work systematically;
- generalize and conjecture;
- explain their thinking and offer proofs of their findings.

Work systematically

Mathematicians want to know whether they have found all the possible solutions. They want to understand all the different representations of a mathematical idea or concept. As an example, how might learners approach writing out pairs of numbers that add to 12.

Some children would approach this in a fairly haphazard way, starting with $10 + 2$, say, and then maybe moving on to $6 + 6$. Other children will take a much more systematic approach. They will come up with the following solution:

$$12 + 0 = 12$$
$$11 + 1 = 12$$
$$10 + 2 = 12$$
$$9 + 3 = 12$$
$$8 + 4 = 12$$
$$7 + 5 = 12$$

$$6 + 6 = 12$$
$$(5 + 7 = 12)$$

They are unlikely to continue further as they will appreciate that $7 + 5$ is equivalent to $5 + 7$, and so on. So now they have seven different ways of making 12.

Generalize and conjecture

Following on from the above activity, the mathematical child may then try to generalize this by thinking how many ways can you make 11? They may conjecture that it should be less than 7, because 11 is smaller than 12.

$$11 + 0 = 11$$
$$10 + 1 = 11$$
$$9 + 2 = 11$$
$$8 + 3 = 11$$
$$7 + 4 = 11$$
$$6 + 5 = 11$$

Indeed, the number of ways is less than 7; in fact, now there are only 6 ways. Might we then predict that for 13 there will be 8 ways?

Proof and explanation

The final stage here would be to explain the thinking and reasoning behind the conjecture and to prove if that thinking was correct. In this way, a mathematician will explore the initial problem systematically and then try to generalize their findings in order to come up with a connection or relationship between different scenarios.

Gilderdale suggested a template for maths lessons that would help children to develop these mathematical characteristics and their mathematical thinking. This template consists of four elements:

● Promoting a conjecturing atmosphere
● Low-threshold/high-ceiling tasks
● Modelling behaviour
● Whole-class discussion.

Promoting a conjecturing atmosphere

> In mathematics the art of proposing a question must be held of higher value than solving it.
>
> Georg Cantor, German mathematician
> and inventor of Set Theory (1962)

Establishing an enquiry-based classroom, where learners are encouraged to ask questions and to take risks will benefit all involved, whether they have learning difficulties or not. For the struggling learner, the idea that mistakes are not just tolerated but positively celebrated will encourage them to 'have a go' rather than sit fearfully at the back of the class. Plenty of discussion and sharing of thoughts and ideas will lead to a more collaborative approach, where children support each other. For this atmosphere to work, all participants need to feel valued and safe in the knowledge that their ideas will be listened to and discussed without fear of ridicule. Problems need to be designed so that learners with maths difficulties have time to think and that other learners have the opportunity to explore the problem further and in greater depth.

The value of questioning should not be underestimated here – both on the part of the learner and the teacher. Boaler (2013) emphasizes the value of questioning as a means of encouraging the learner to explain their thinking and to defend their reasoning. Many children find this difficult, as 'they just know' the answer. Deep questioning in this way can help them to clarify their understanding and also acts as an assessment opportunity for the teacher to ascertain whether the child has deep or merely superficial understanding of the concept. This can be simply achieved by asking the question: 'Are you sure?' As teachers, we tend to ask this question when the learner has made a mistake, but by asking it when the learner is correct, we encourage them to explain their reasoning and to present an argument to support their thinking.

Low-threshold/high-ceiling tasks

The selection of task is key to making sure that all learners have the opportunity to develop their mathematical understanding as much as possible. Problems should be chosen that are accessible to everyone regardless of ability, but which also offer opportunities for exploration and development of depth of understanding. Such tasks are naturally inclusive because everyone can access them, so they are non-threatening for the dyscalculic learner and will help to reduce their maths anxiety.

For example, in the four 4s problem (detailed in Chapter 9) the children are asked to express every number from 1 to 20, using four 4s and any number operation.

This is a good example of a low-threshold/high-ceiling task, as some of the numbers are much easier to make than others:

$$16 = 4 + 4 + 4 + 4$$

So every child can access this problem and some will be able to take it much further than others. Visit www.nrich.org for a very good source of these types of problems, as is Jo Boaler's website: www.youcubed.com.

Modelling behaviour

I am a firm believer that some of the best teachers of maths are the ones who have struggled with it in the past, as they can empathize with a learner's difficulties and may have a better insight into their misconceptions. However, it is very important to show the learner that we as teachers are excited by maths, that we enjoy maths, and that we present it in a way that inspires and fosters curiosity around the subject. Maths really is an incredibly rich, challenging subject with a natural beauty that at times is simply breathtaking. We are doing our children a great disservice if we do not convey that to them.

Whole-class discussion

Discussion should be an integral and ongoing part of the lesson, initially to explore ideas, then to modify and highlight strategies before sharing solutions and proofs. In his constructivist approach to learning, Vygotsky (1978) found that children construct their understanding through social interaction. This is such an important aspect of all lessons, as it gives everyone the opportunity to voice their ideas and their questions and provides a supportive and safe environment for discussing different strategies and approaches.

Gilderdale (2007) also advocates 'HOTS not MOTS', which stands for 'Higher Order Thinking Skills' not 'More of the Same'. Certainly, in my experience at school, if I found something hard, the teacher would give me more examples to practise on. This 'more of the same' approach is hardly ever helpful, as it reinforces the feeling of failure and does not provide the learner with other potentially more fruitful ways of looking at the problem. Encouraging higher-order thinking skills develops number sense and will help the learner to access other ways of solving the problem.

Learning styles

Different people have different ways of approaching maths problems. Some people are very logical and structured in their approach while others are more intuitive and flexible.

These learning styles have been recognized for many years and have been labelled in various ways. In 1908, they were termed geometers and algebraists by Boltevskii, the algebraists being logical and structured and the geometers being more flexible and intuitive. In 1986, Sharma renamed the algebraists as quantitative and the geometers as qualitative. A perhaps more accessible description was offered by Bath et al. in 1986, who labelled these two styles as inchworms and grasshoppers (see Table 8.1). In 1992, Chinn detailed these traits with reference to the three stages of solving a problem.

Is one style better than the other? Well, it depends what you are doing. Children who feel insecure about an aspect of maths will tend towards an inchworm approach. Even children who are naturally grasshoppers will become inchworms if they are too far out of their comfort zone. So what we are really looking for here is flexibility in approach and an awareness of when to favour one style over another. From a teaching point of view, it is important that you are aware of individual preferences and of different learning styles so that you can match your teaching and any intervention programme accordingly.

I have long debated with practitioners as to which style of approach most suits learners who are really struggling with maths. Some practitioners would advocate teaching one method that works and encouraging the struggling learner to only use that one method. The argument is that it is less confusing for the learner, as they only

Table 8.1 Cognitive styles of the inchworm and the grasshopper

	Inchworm	Grasshopper
Analysing and identifying the problem	Focuses on parts, attends to detail and separates	Holistic, forms concepts and puts together
	Objective of looking at facts to determine useful formulae	Objective of looking at facts to determine an estimate of answer or range of restrictions
Methods of solving the problem	Formula, recipe orientated	Controlled exploration
	Constrained focusing using a single method or serially ordered steps along one route, generally in one direction, forward	Flexible focusing using multi-methods or paths, frequently occurring simultaneously, generally reversing or working back from an answer and trying new routes
	Uses numbers exactly as given	Adjusts, breaks down/builds up numbers to make an easier calculation
	Tending to add and multiply; resists subtraction and division	Tending to subtract
	Tending to use paper and pencil to compute	Tending to perform all calculation mentally
	Verification unlikely; if done, uses same procedure or method	Likely to verify; probably uses alternative procedure or method

Source: Bath et al. (1986).

have to remember one procedure. Others would argue that it is better to give the struggling learner a range of methods, so that they can choose the one that suits them best. In this instance, the learner has to remember more than one way of solving a problem, but the emphasis is more on understanding.

The problem with providing one method only is that we are limiting the child's understanding of maths and also not giving them the opportunity to develop their sense of number. In a worst-case scenario, we are actually making maths harder for them, as they are not being exposed to the 'easier' way of solving a problem. For example, if the learner is presented with 3000 – 287, what are their options?

For the learner who has been taught one method, there is just the one way of doing this. They will probably have been shown how to write this as a column subtraction, and they will have to decompose and regroup in the following way:

3000	2000	900	90	10
– 287	–		200	80	7
????	2000	700	10	3

And then regroup to give the answer $2000 + 700 + 10 + 3 = 2713$.

Alternatively, if they had been shown alternative methods they may well see the problem like this:

$$
\begin{array}{r}
3000 \\
- 287 \\
\hline
???? \\
\end{array}
$$

Let's change that problem, as it is quite tricky, by taking 1 away from both numbers. So now the question has been simplified to

$$
\begin{array}{r}
2999 \\
- 286 \\
\hline
2713 \\
\end{array}
$$

We can do this as long as we understand what we are looking at when we are subtracting one number from another. We are considering the relative positions of the numbers to each other on a number line, in other words the difference between the two numbers:

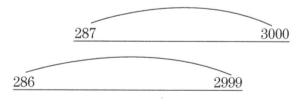

The distance between the two numbers has not changed, because we have simply moved them both one place to the left on the number line.

So, by limiting learners who are struggling to just one method, we are effectively 'backing them into a corner' where they are forced to use a method that may not be the most efficient or elegant method or even the most easily understood.

This was brought home to me while training a group of teachers in what is meant by mastery in maths. We were looking at how to calculate 36 × 175 ÷ 63 in our heads, as an example of what mastery in multiplication and division can look like. The teachers came up with several different methods.

Method 1: Long multiplication and division

175 × 36, using the grid method:

	100	70	5	
30	3000	2100	150	
6	600	420	30	
	3600	2520	180	**6300**

Then, 6300 ÷ 63 = 100.

Not quite so easy to do in your head.

Method 2: Partitioning

Take the 175 and partition it into 100 and 75. Now we can easily multiply 36 by 100, to give us 3600 and then we can use our number sense to work out that 36 × 75 will be $\frac{3}{4}$ of 3600, because 75 is $\frac{3}{4}$ of 100.

So 3/4 of 3600 is (3600 ÷ 4) × 3 = 2700.

So now we know that 36 × 175 = 3600 + 2700 = 6300.

We then divide 6300 by 63 as before to give us 100.

Possible to do in your head but still quite demanding on working memory.

Method 3: Doubling and halving

36 × 175 ÷ 63

These are difficult numbers to work with but I know that if I am multiplying two numbers together, I can halve one and double the other and the result will be the same. So let's try that and see if it makes the numbers easier to work with.

Halve 36 and double 175 gives:

18 × 350

Let's do it again.

Halve 18 and double 350 gives:

9×700

This is easier: $9 \times 700 = 6300$

Then proceed as before, by dividing by 63 to give the answer 100.

Method 4: Use number sense

Look at how the numbers relate to each other and think what they have in common:

$36 \times 175 \div 63$

$\dfrac{36 \times 175}{63}$ can be written as: $\dfrac{(9 \times 4) \times (25 \times 7)}{(9 \times 7)}$

In this method we are looking for how these numbers relate to each other and what we can and can't do with them. Now we can see that 9/9 = 1 and also 7/7 = 1 and we know that multiplying by 1 has no effect on the product. Therefore, we can cancel out the 9s and the 7s, leaving us simply with

$4 \times 25 = 100$

This is much quicker and much easier to do in your head.

When I carried out this activity with a group of primary teachers, they collectively came up with all of these methods, but many of them had not considered any other method than the one they first thought of. Cries of 'I would never have thought of doing it that way' could be heard throughout the room. Many of the teachers felt that the task was too difficult to do in their heads and had actually given up. However, when they saw the solutions they all had their particular favourite – the one method that they understood more than the others. These favourite methods varied from teacher to teacher, but they had all been exposed to a new way of thinking and were now equipped with multiple ways of solving similar problems in the future.

Clearly, the situation is exactly the same for the struggling learner. We want to equip them with different ways of solving problems, so that they can find ones that they like and, most importantly, understand. This will help them not to give up and to try different ways to solve problems that may be very hard to do if you only have one method (e.g. the grid method) at your disposal.

Key facts and derived facts

In 1994, Gray and Tall of the University of Warwick published a paper entitled 'Duality, ambiguity and flexibility: a proceptual view of simple arithmetic'. In this paper, they made a very compelling argument that children who are less able in maths are actually doing a harder version of maths than their more able peers. The maths that the more able children do is an easier version because they are able to use number flexibly and can derive new facts from known facts. These children understand how to combine mathematical process and concept, which the authors term 'procept'.

In essence, less able children follow a procedure, often underpinned by very poor understanding of the mathematical concept. Hiebert and Lefevre describe conceptual knowledge as:

> . . . a connected web . . . a network in which the linking relationships are as prominent as the discrete pieces of information . . . a unit of conceptual knowledge cannot be an isolated piece of information; by definition it is part of conceptual knowledge only if the holder recognises its relationship to other pieces of information.
>
> (Hiebert and Lefevre 1986: 3–4)

The word 'procept' refers to the amalgam of concept and process represented by the same symbol. For example, we can refer to the procept 6. In what ways can we think of 6? What do we know about 6?

> 6 can be the number of items in a set, and would be the last number that we count when there are 6 objects in a set. It is also $3 + 3, 4 + 2, 5 + 1, 7 - 1, 2 \times 3, 8 - 2$, etc.

A child with good understanding of the procept 6 will know that all these different symbols represent 6 and they can use these versions of 6 according to the circumstances of the question.

So, proceptual thinking is all about flexibility, having a good sense of number. It is about understanding how numbers relate to each other, how to decompose and recompose numbers, and knowing what we can and can't do with number.

In their study, Gray and Tall selected a cohort of 72 children between the ages of 7 and 12 years who had been grouped by their teachers as above average, average or below average. Gray and Tall presented the children with addition and subtraction questions that were in one of three categories:

Addition problems

(A) Single-digit addition with a sum of 10 or less (e.g. 6 + 3, 3 + 5)
(B) Addition of a single-digit number to a teen number, the sum being 20 or less than 20 (e.g. 18 + 2, 13 + 5)
(C) Addition of two single-digit numbers with a sum between 11 and 20 (e.g. 4 + 7, 9 + 8).

Subtraction problems

(A) Single-digit subtraction (e.g. 8 – 2)
(B) Subtraction of a single-digit number from one between 10 and 20 (e.g. 16 – 3, 15 – 9)
(C) Subtraction of a two-digit number between 10 and 20 from another two-digit number (e.g. 16 – 10, 19 – 17).

Of the children that achieved an above-average score:

9% counted on
used 30% known facts
used 61% derived facts

Of the children that achieved a below-average score:

72% counted on
22% counted all
used 6% known facts
used 0% derived facts

The below-average children nearly always favoured count-back as the procedure for taking away. For example, 18 – 15 was calculated by the long-winded process of counting back 15 places from 18, an inefficient procedure that is prone to error. The above-average children selected the more efficient strategy, from the range of strategies in their mathematical tool box, and counted up from 15 to 18, as they were able to appreciate that these two numbers are close together. However, for 18 – 3 they counted back, as this was the more efficient method – there are only a few steps to count back.

The ability to think flexibly and to derive new facts from known facts greatly reduces the load on memory. So more able children appreciate that they don't need to remember everything because they can generate new facts from key known facts. In contrast, the memory load of less able children is overwhelming and because they have such poor use of procept, they are forced to rely on recall of set procedures that can often be inappropriate and laborious.

This study is very significant in terms of its implication for learners with specific maths difficulties. It shows us that we need to help these learners to look for links and connection, to generalize their learning, so that they can derive new facts from key facts – in other words, to develop their number sense.

Metacognition

The Rose Review (2009) defined metacognition as understanding one's own learning processes. Many practitioners refer to metacognition as 'thinking about your thinking'. Developing metacognitive skills in children gives them ownership of their learning and helps them to understand what strategies work for them. It encourages them to think more deeply about their learning and this in turn helps to develop their cognitive abilities.

Fogarty (1994) suggests that metacognition is a process that has three distinct phases. In order to be effective thinkers, students must do the following:

- *Plan*: Before starting to solve a maths problem, the learner needs to plan a course of action.
- *Monitor*: During problem-solving, monitor progress. Is their plan working? Have they selected the best strategy?
- *Evaluate*: On completion of the task, evaluate how successful the approach was.

Teachers can facilitate the development of metacognitive skills by asking questions of the learners and by also encouraging them to question themselves. In the 1980s, Schoenfeld conducted an experiment that showed that learners performed better if they asked themselves simple questions, such as: 'What am I doing right now?' and 'Why am I doing it?'

So, during each of the above phases, learners should ask themselves the following types of question:

- *Planning*: What is the question asking me to do? What should I do first? Have I seen a problem like this before? What strategies worked for that problem? Can I apply them here?
- *Monitoring*: How am I getting on? Is this strategy working? What other methods could I use? Am I getting nearer to the answer?
- *Evaluation*: Did I solve the problem? Did I use the most efficient strategy? Could I have done anything better? Was there something that I did not understand? Could I apply what I have done here to other problems in the future?

How to help learners think about their thinking

Prompt the learner to question themselves at each of the three stages. Discuss strategies with them, and let them write down their ideas or strategies if they want to. Ask them to assess their approach once the problem has been solved and evaluate how effective it was. Give the learner tasks that have more than one solution and more than one method of being solved.

Questions that help to develop an awareness of how you learn include:

- What did you learn?
- How did you learn it?
- Did you find anything very difficult?
- Did you find anything very easy?
- How did you do this task?

Questions that help to develop an awareness of attitudes and feelings include:

- What did you like from this task?
- What was good about this task?
- What was not so good about this task?

Questions that help to develop an awareness of setting goals include:

- Could you have done anything better?
- What is your next target?
- What will help you to achieve your next target?

Metacognition training programmes

There are several training programmes designed to develop metacognitive awareness. Kramarski et al. (2010) found that learners who had been supported by metacognitive questioning experienced greater gains than children who had not been exposed to metacognitive questioning. It was also found that their maths anxiety was reduced.

IMPROVE: Mevarech and Kamarski (1997) developed a training programme which they called IMPROVE. Using this programme, learners are taught to use a series of metacognitive questions during maths tasks. The teaching steps involved make up the acronym IMPROVE:

> Introducing new concepts
> Metacognitive questioning
> Practising
> Reviewing
> Obtaining mastery
> Verification
> Enrichment

WWW&H: Veenman (1998) formulated the WWW&H rule for training metacognition, referring to instructions about what metacognitive activities should be executed. WWW&H stands for:

> When
> Why
> What
> How.

MASTER: Van Luit and Naglieri (1999) developed a programme called MASTER for teaching multiplication and division strategies to children with specific learning difficulties.

Results from these training programmes show that all learners, particularly those with learning difficulties in maths, can benefit from some form of metacognitive training All of these approaches have been found to be successful in helping learners to improve their problem-solving and reasoning.

Growth mindset

> You must learn to fail intelligently. Failing is one of the greatest arts in the world. One fails forward to success.
>
> Thomas Edison

Growth mindset refers to a learner's attitude to their maths ability and potential in maths. Learners with a growth mindset believe that they can improve their maths ability. In contrast, learners with a fixed mindset believe that their ability in maths is never going to change, no matter what they do.

This is not a new concept. Virgil, one of ancient Rome's greatest poets, stated *Possunt quia posse videntur*, which translates as:

> They can, because they think they can.

However, there has been a widely held myth in maths that you are born with the innate skill of either being good or bad at it. This is perpetuated by some parents, who by claiming that they were 'terrible at maths' when they were at school, seek to comfort their children when they do poorly in maths – thus giving the impression that being bad at maths is hereditary, in just the same way as having blonde hair and freckles: it is what you were born with and there is nothing you can do about it. In her book *Mindset: The new psychology of success* (2006), Carol Dweck dispels this mathematical myth through exploring the power of our mindset. She explains why it's not just our abilities and talent that bring us success, but whether we have adopted a fixed or growth mindset in our approach. With the right mindset, children can improve their motivation and attainment. She states:

> Motivation is the most important factor in determining whether you succeed in the long run. What I mean by motivation is not only the desire to achieve, but also the love of learning, the love of challenge and the ability to thrive on obstacles. These are the greatest gifts we can give our students.
>
> (Dweck 2006: 61)

Dweck (2000) also highlighted four beliefs about ability, success, praise, and confidence:

1   **The belief that students with high ability are more likely to display 'mastery-oriented' qualities.** Somewhat surprisingly, many learners who are considered as being very able in maths do not have a robust belief in their own ability. These learners are often anxious about failing and their self-confidence can easily be shattered in the face of obstacles that they find hard to overcome (Leggett 1985).

2   **The belief that success in school directly fosters mastery-oriented qualities.** It may seem that learners are spurred on by their success, but in reality this success does not affect their ability to cope with failures or setbacks (Diener and Dweck 1978, 1980).

3   **The belief that praise, particularly praising a student's intelligence, encourages mastery-oriented qualities.** This is a very pervasive belief and many parents, myself included, will have praised our children for being clever. This in fact does little to boost the child's confidence in the long term, since when they find something that they don't succeed in they equate this with being stupid. Consequently, they are less likely to take risks and will be ill equipped to deal with setbacks (Mueller and Dweck 1998).

4   **The belief that students' confidence in their intelligence is the key to mastery-oriented qualities.** Many seemingly confident children do not possess resilience in the face of adversity and are fearful of their intelligence being tested. They are reluctant to explain their reasoning for fear of making a mistake or of appearing not to understand (Henderson and Dweck 1990).

Boaler (2013) relates the concepts of a growth mindset and fixed mindset to the teaching of mathematics. Some people believe that maths ability is a gift, something that we are born with. We either can or cannot do maths. This is very much a fixed mindset and one that can perpetuate into adulthood. However, other people may struggle with maths but don't feel that the difficulties are insurmountable. These learners are prepared to 'have a go', they persist and learn from their mistakes, and are encouraged by seeing the progress that their peers have made.

Growth mindset people 'can because they think they can'.
Fixed Mindset people 'can't because they think they can't'.

This has huge implications for the dyscalculic learner who needs to believe that they will be able to overcome their difficulties with maths. The statements in Table 8.2 detail how each of these mindsets manifests itself.

Table 8.2 The growth mindset and fixed mindset

Growth mindset	Fixed mindset
Belief that intelligence is not fixed – my intelligence can be improved through learning	Believing that talent is static – you can only be successful if you are naturally talented
Seeing mistakes as a positive – something to learn from	Preferring to stay in their comfort zone – avoiding challenging situations
Thriving on challenge and being self-confident	Avoiding challenge
Not giving up easily – having resilience in their approach to maths	Giving up easily. Anxiety about making mistakes – belief that maths is all about getting the answer right
Believing that hard work pays off – effort will bring success	Being self-conscious in front of their peers – won't offer a solution in public for fear of looking 'stupid'
Reflecting on strategies that work for them – developing metacognitive awareness	Not reflecting on what strategies have helped them to learn or to move on
Having learning goals and using feedback to improve	Staying with easy performance goals and enjoying being praised for doing well

Children can be taught how to rephrase fixed mindset beliefs into growth mindset beliefs. The SWAP table shown in Box 8.2 provides some examples

---

Box 8.2: SWAP table

SWAP I am stupid	for	I can't do this yet
SWAP This is too hard	for	This may take a little while
SWAP I wish I was as clever as my classmate	for	I am going to work out how they got the answer
SWAP I have never done this before – I have not been shown how to do it	for	What has worked in the past that may help me here? Have I done anything similar?

SWAP I have got an answer, so I have finished	for	Am I sure this is correct – can I check it using a different method?
SWAP I will never need to know this area of maths when I leave school	for	Working this out will help me to become better at solving problems

Teachers can also monitor their thoughts and comments to promote a more growth mindset environment for their learners (see Table 8.3).

Table 8.3 Growth and fixed mindset approaches

Growth mindset approaches	Fixed mindset approaches
Praising effort and strategies	Praising correct answers
Feedback emphasizing effort and application	Feedback emphasizing achievement
Focus on developing self-confidence	False or empty praise
Developing intelligence and skills	Recording intelligence and skills – over-assessing
Promoting independent learning and ownership of tasks	Directing pupils to tasks
Focus on learning and understanding	Focus on results and performance

How can we develop this motivation for learning?

The goal here is to develop learners who are successful. Successful learners will be the ones who love learning, who enjoy the effort of a real challenge, and don't give up easily when things are tough.

- *Growth mindset/incremental learners.* These successful learners have a growth mindset and believe that everyone can achieve with the right level of effort and guidance. They are more focused on the learning than on appearing clever. They are resilient and will keep on trying to solve the problem even if they find it very difficult.
- *Fixed mindset/entity learners.* These learners are much less resilient and will avoid challenges. They like praise that makes them feel smarter, but in fact this type of praise only serves to underpin their vulnerabilities and does not help build a robust self-esteem. Robust self-esteem is developed over time and comes

from being immersed in a problem that is at the edge of your comfort zone and sticking with this problem until it has been solved. In that way you have, through your own efforts, achieved something of value. There is little value in staying well within your comfort zone and solving a simple problem.

How can we help fixed mindset learners to adopt a more growth mindset approach?

- Praise the learner in the right way.
- Praise effort, resilience, and hard work – not intelligence (i.e. do not tell children how clever they are).
- Concentrate children on improving their own performance (in small achievable steps) and not on comparing themselves to their peers.
- Remind children that if the work is not hard, they are not learning at the optimum level. It is good to feel challenged in maths.
- Stress that intelligence is not fixed, but is improved by effort and hard work.

It can helpful to provide learners with examples of people who have achieved success through a 'can do' growth mindset approach. Albert Einstein learned to talk later than many other children and was thought of as being 'backward'. He had to leave school at 15 because of his disruptive behaviour. He failed to get a job as a teacher, but went on the win the Nobel Prize for Physics. Winston Churchill had a difficult childhood and made little progress at school. However, he went on to become Prime Minister and was widely credited with leading Britain to victory in the Second World War.

Myth busting in maths

In order to support the idea of a growth mindset, it would be opportune here to dispel a few of the more persistent myths surrounding maths.

You need to do it quickly. Being fast at maths does not always equate to being good at maths. Sometimes if it takes you longer to learn something, it means that you have a deeper understanding of it.

You need to do it mentally. Although there is no doubt that it is beneficial to be able to perform calculations mentally, it is not imperative that we do so. Learners with working memory difficulties will find mental calculation very challenging and this can be a real barrier for them. For these learners, it may be much more beneficial to write down their approach and the calculations that need to be performed rather than having to keep all the information in their heads.

You need to do it correctly. This is a very common misconception. Clearly our aim is to make sure that learners can get the right answer but along the way they are bound to make mistakes and this is all part of the learning process. Mistakes provide a great opportunity for learning. So we need to help children to take risks and not be afraid of failing. Try to get them to think along the lines of 'I can't do this *yet*', rather than simply 'I can't do this'.

References

Bath, J.B., Chinn, S.J. and Knox, D.E. (1986) *The Test of Cognitive Style in Mathematics*. East Aurora, NY: Slosson.

Boaler, J. (2013) *How to Learn Math* [retrieved from: https://lagunita.stanford.edu/courses/Education/EDUC115N/How_to_Learn_Math/about; accessed 19 September 2016].

Bruner, J. (1960) *The Process of Education*. Cambridge, MA: Harvard University Press.

Cantor, G. (1962) *Of Men and Numbers*. New York: Dodd, Mead & Co.

Chinn, S. (1992) Individual diagnosis and cognitive style, in T.R. Miles and E. Miles (eds.) *Dyslexia and Mathematics*. London: Routledge.

Diener, C.I. and Dweck, C.S. (1978) An analysis of learned helplessness: continuous changes in performance, strategy and achievement cognitions following failure, *Journal of Personality and Social Psychology*, 36: 451–62.

Diener, C.I. and Dweck, C.S. (1980) An analysis of learned helplessness, II: the processing of success, *Journal of Personality and Social Psychology*, 39: 940–52.

Dweck, C.S. (2000) *Self-theories: Their role in motivation, personality, and development*. Hove: Psychology Press.

Dweck, C. (2006) *Mindset: The new psychology of success*. New York: Ballantine Books.

Fogarty, R. (1994) *How to Teach for Metacognition.* Palatine, IL: IRI Skylight Publishing.

Fuchs, L., Fuchs, D., Powell, S., Seethaler, P., Cirino, P. and Fletcher, J. (2008) Intensive intervention for students with mathematics disabilities: seven principles of effective practice, *Learning Disability Quarterly*, 31(2): 79–92.

Gilderdale, C. (2007) Generating curiosity in mathematics learning, Council of Boards of School Education in India Conference 'Addressing Core Issues and Concerns in Science and Mathematics', Rishikesh, India.

Gray, E. and Tall, D. (1994) Duality, ambiguity and flexibility: a proceptual view of simple arithmetic, *Journal for Research in Mathematics Education*, 26(2): 115–41.

Gudder, S. (1993) *A Mathematical Journey.* New York: McGraw-Hill.

Henderson, V.L. and Dweck, C.S. (1990) Achievement and motivation in adolescence: a new model and data, in S. Feldman and G. Elliott (eds.) *At the Threshold: The developing adolescent.* Cambridge, MA: Harvard University Press.

Hiebert, J. and Lefevre, P. (1986) Procedural and conceptual knowledge, in J. Hiebert (ed.) *Conceptual and Procedural Knowledge: The case of mathematics* (pp. 1–27). Hillsdale, NJ: Lawrence Erlbaum.

Kramarski, B., Weisse, I. and Kololshi-Minsker, I. (2010) How can self-regulated learning support the problem solving of third-grade students with mathematics anxiety?, *Mathematics Education*, 42(2): 179–93.

Leggett, E. (1985) Children's entity and incremental theories of intelligence: Relationships to achievement behavior. Paper presented at the annual meeting of the Eastern Psychological Association, Boston, MA.

Mevarech, Z. and Kamarski, B. (1997) IMPROVE: a multidimensional method for teaching mathematics in heterogeneous classrooms, *American Educational Research Journal*, 34(2): 365–94.

Mueller, C. and Dweck, C. (1998) Praise for intelligence can undermine children's motivation and performance, *Journal of Personality and Social Psychology*, 75(1): 33–52.

Rose, J. (2009) *Identifying and Teaching Children and Young People with Dyslexia and Literacy Difficulties* (The Rose Review) [retrieved from www.interventionsforliteracy.org.uk/assets/Uploads/The-Rose-Report-June-2009.pdf; accessed 22 May 2017].

Schoenfeld, A. (1987) What's all the fuss about metacognition?, in A. Schoenfeld (ed.) *Cognitive Science and Mathematics Education* (pp. 189–215). Hillsdale, NJ: Lawrence Erlbaum.

Sharma, M.C. (1986) Dyscalculia and other learning problems in arithmetic: a historical perspective, *Focus on Learning Problems in Mathematics*, 8(3/4): 7–45.

Sharma, M. (2009) *Mathematics Curriculum, Core Concepts, Skills and Procedures* [retrieved from: www.info@mathematicsforall. org; accessed 17 September 2016].

Van Luit, J. and Naglieri, J. (1999) Effectiveness of the MASTER program for teaching special children multiplication and division, *Journal of Learning Disabilities*, 32(2): 98–107.

Veenman, M. (1998) Knowledge and skills that are relevant to math tasks, in A. Andeweg, J.E.H. van Luit, M.V.J. Veenman and P.C.M. Vendel (eds.) *Hulp bij leerproblemen: Rekenen-wiskunde* (pp. G0050.1–13). Alphen a/d Rijn: Kluwer.

Vygotsky, L.S. (1978) *Mind in Society: The development of higher psychological processes*. Cambridge, MA: Harvard University Press.

Manipulatives

An objects to Think With.

Papert (1980)

Manipulatives are any physical objects that can be used to model a mathematical idea or concept. They are by far the most effective way to support learners with specific difficulties in maths. Used in the correct way they can help a child move away from immature counting strategies and can help them to develop their number sense. Stein and Bovalino (2001: 356) stated:

> Manipulatives can be important tools in helping students to think and reason in more meaningful ways. By giving students concrete ways to compare and operate on quantities, such manipulatives as pattern blocks, tiles, and cubes can contribute to the development of well-grounded, interconnected understandings of mathematical ideas.

We have understood the merit of using manipulatives for many years. Piaget (1952) recommended manipulatives as a way of embodying mathematical concepts. Gattegno and Cuisenaire developed the widely used Cuisenaire rods in 1954 and Dienes (1969) developed his base materials (base ten in particular) as a way of helping children to understand concepts such as place value. Variability in selection of manipulatives is important so that the learner understands that the concept can be represented in multiple ways and so that they don't become too reliant on any single resource. By using a variety of manipulatives, the learner will be able to 'see' the maths and will be able to explore the concept through handling and manipulating the resources.

Manipulatives should be made available at all times and regular use will help to link the abstract maths to the concrete. In this way, learners are more likely to persevere with a problem and to work more independently. By working in pairs or small groups, learners will also develop their use of mathematical language to explain their thinking and reasoning.

Misuse of manipulatives

It is important that manipulatives are used correctly. They should not be used as a 'crutch' for children who are struggling, just to help them follow a procedure, nor should they be *only* given to children who are struggling. The learner should be given the opportunity to select the manipulative that they feel helps them the most, but should also be encouraged to work with a variety of manipulatives to develop their understanding and flexibility of thought. One of the greatest misuses of manipulatives is that they are often taken away far too soon and this leads to maths becoming abstract and inaccessible. Many learners develop maths anxiety at the age of 6 or 7 years and this tends to coincide with when they move from Key Stage 1 to Key Stage 2, when many manipulatives are removed from classrooms.

Good use of manipulatives

Let the children play with the resources, particularly if they have not used them before. This time for free play can really help the learner to understand how they can use the manipulative to model different mathematical scenarios. Make sure that a wide variety of resources are readily accessible at all times and are available throughout Key Stage 1 and Key Stage 2, and beyond as and when necessary.

Children who are struggling with maths need to be encouraged to engage in active guided discovery. So they need to move the materials, talk about them, and represent the concept in different ways with different materials. This should be guided by the teacher, who responds to learners' comments and helps them to discover the next conceptual step in the learning for themselves through the use of the materials. This deep exploration of the materials means that the children can visualize the materials and the maths more easily when the materials are not present.

Choice of manipulative

This often depends on the particular learning style of the child. Inch-worms will prefer *discrete materials*, objects such as counters, coins, plastic animals, glass nuggets, cubes, base ten equipment, and Numicon. In contrast, grasshoppers will prefer *continuous materials*, objects such as Cuisenaire rods, Stern blocks, and number lines.

The Internet has many sites where you can access virtual manipulatives. The following is a particularly good one: http://nlvm.usu.edu/en/nav/vlibrary.html.

Mathematical tool box

The following is a suggested, though not exhaustive, list of resources that will help to support children with specific difficulties in maths. In fact, they will support all maths learners, whatever their ability. It is best, however, if a child has their own personal set of resources. This promotes independence and also results in the child being more likely to look after their maths tool box.

- A set of dot pattern cards from 1 to 10
- A set of digit cards from 1 to 10, 1 to 20 or 1 to 100, depending on what is appropriate for the child's stage of learning
- Number bond cards with bonds of all numbers up to and including ten
- A set of memory cards detailing any information that needs to be rehearsed on a daily basis
- Laminated number square: this can be 1 to 100 or 100 to 1
- Arrow cards for place value
- Ten frames
- Double-sided counters
- Place value counters
- Paper strips and paper squares
- Number lines or number tracks
- Laminated blank number lines
- Squared paper
- Calculator

- Multilink cubes
- 0–6 dice
- 0–9 dice
- 10 or 20 bead string
- Whiteboard, pen, and cloth
- Scissors

Activities to develop number sense

Cuisenaire rods

Staircase game

The resources required include: a set of Cuisenaire rods, 1–10, one of each colour and a 1–10 dice. The aim of the game is for the players to replicate the staircase pattern shown in Figure 9.1.

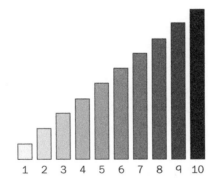

1 2 3 4 5 6 7 8 9 10

Figure 9.1 Cuisenaire rods. Rods are coloured 1 = white, 2 = red, 3 = light green, 4 = pink, 5 = yellow, 6 = dark green, 7 = black, 8 = brown, 9 = blue, 10 = orange

Each player takes it in turn to roll the dice and place the corresponding Cuisenaire rod on the table to create the staircase sequence. So, if player one throws a 5, they place the yellow rod on the table. If player two then throws an 8, they have to decide how far to the right of the 5 to place the brown rod in order to make a Cuisenaire staircase. If a number is repeated when the dice is thrown, that player misses a turn. The player who places the last rod in the sequence is the winner.

This game helps learners to appreciate how the numbers 1–10 relate to each other. The staircase pattern shows them that each number in the sequence 1–10 is one more than the previous number, and indicates where the numbers belong on a number line.

Rod sandwiches

The resources required include: a set of Cuisenaire rods. This game will help learners to understand how to decompose and recompose numbers to ten.

To start, the learner selects two rods of the same length which are used to represent the bread in the sandwich. They then explore which other rods can be used to fill the sandwich. They can select as many rods as they like to fill the sandwich. Figure 9.2 uses two '8' rods to show the different 'fillings' that make 8.

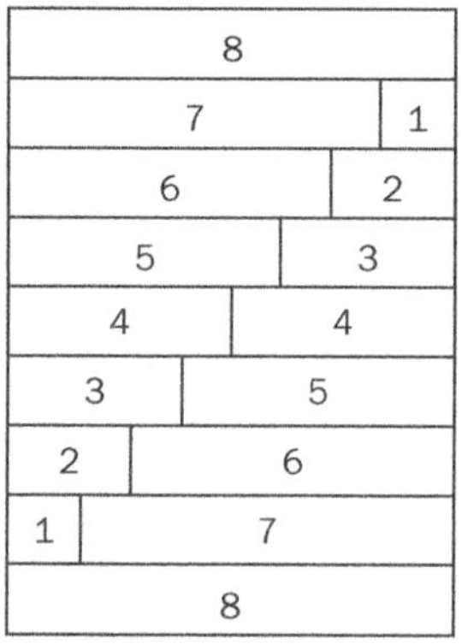

Figure 9.2 Example rod sandwich

Rod relationships

The resources required include: a set of Cuisenaire rods, a rod track, and a centimetre ruler.

Select a length between 10 and 20 cm, say 16 cm. The learner can then explore how many different ways a length of 16 cm can be made by joining two Cuisenaire rods end to end along a centimetre ruler or rod track. They can record their solutions using pictures and equations; for example, 9 cm + 7 cm = 16 cm. This activity can be extended by increasing the number of Cuisenaire rods joined together to make the length selected; for example, 8 cm + 6 cm + 4 cm = 18 cm.

Five frames and ten frames

Five frame talk

The resources required include: a five frame and five counters.

Ask the learner to show a given number on the frame using the requisite number of counters; for example, three counters to depict the number 3. They can place the counters anywhere they like on the five frame (see Figure 9.3).

Figure 9.3 Counters on a five frame

They now have to describe to you what they can see. You can prompt them by asking questions such as:

'How many spaces can you see?'
'Is three less than five? How do you know?'
'What numbers is three made from?' (1 and 1 and 1 or 2 and 1, depending on the arrangement of counters)

Repeat this with different numbers of counters and try to encourage the learner to see how these numbers relate to 5, as the aim is to introduce 5 as the 'benchmark' number. If they can see how a number relates to 5 and later on to 10, they will begin to develop a deeper sense of number and how numbers relate to each other. It will also help them when they are placing numbers on a number line.

Ten frame talk

A five frame talk can be extended to a ten frame talk and exploring how larger numbers can be arranged on a ten frame. The resources required include: a ten frame and ten counters.

In Frame 1, 7 can be viewed as a 5 (top row) and a 2 (bottom row). It can also be viewed as a 4 (first two columns) and a 3 (three final columns in top row).

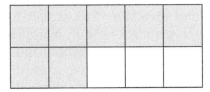

Frame 1

In Frame 2, 7 can be viewed as a 3 (first two columns), another 3 (three final columns in top row), and a 1 (penultimate column in bottom row). Or it could be viewed as a 1 + 3 (top row) and a 2 + 1 (bottom row).

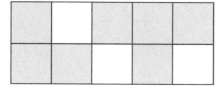

Frame 2

Frame 3 shows different ways of summing to 7 (i.e. 4 + 3 or 2 + 2 + 2 + 1).

Frame 3

The idea is that the learner can explain how they view the number and that they are using either visual clusters or subitizing to 'see' the number rather than counting. You can help them to develop this flexibility of thinking about number by asking them questions to draw out their understanding.

Ten frame match

The resources required include: two blank ten frames and counters. This barrier game for two players is aimed at developing visualization skills and the correct use of mathematical language.

The players sit opposite each other with a barrier in between so that they cannot see each other's frames. The first player arranges some counters on their frame and then the other player has to replicate the arrangement by asking questions. For example: Are there any spaces on the top row? Is the final column full? Are there an odd number of counters? How many spaces are there? The game can be made more difficult by limiting the number of questions.

Numicon games

Numicon is a widely used and very popular system developed by Oxford University Press (see Figure 9.4). It consists of coloured tiles with holes representing 1 to 10, pegs, a peg board, number lines and tracks, and bead strings. The system is compatible with Cuisenaire rods and is designed to help children gain a solid understanding of basic number concepts. There are many games and activities using Numicon, a few of which are highlighted below.

Figure 9.4 Numicon games

Feely bag fun

The resources required include: one set of Numicon tiles from 1 to 10.

Place the Numicon tiles in the bag and ask the learner to feel one of the shapes. Can they describe it to you? How many holes are there? Is it a smooth rectangle? What number do they think it represents? After they have had the chance to describe the tile, get them to remove it from the bag and place it on the table to make the sequence 1–10. Continue feeling and describing the shapes and placing them on the table until the whole sequence 1–10 has been made. Discuss the patterns that they can see.

Numicon rod match

The resources required include: one set of Numicon tiles from 1 to 10 and a set of Cuisenaire rods from 1 to 10. The idea of the game is to match the Cuisenaire rods to the Numicon tiles. This can be done in a variety of ways.

A ten tile can match with an orange 10 rod or with 5 lots of 2 tiles or with 2 lots of 5 tiles. A nine tile can match with the blue 9 rod or a yellow 5 rod and a pink 4 rod.

Dozen discovery

The resources required include: pairs of Numicon tiles that total 12 and a feely bag. This is a game for two players.

One player takes a tile from the feely bag. The other player has to then feel for the matching tile that will make 12. If they are correct, they keep that pair. If they are incorrect, they have to return the tile to the bag and play moves to their opponent. Players keep taking turns until all the pairs have been matched.

This game can be easily varied by changing the target number or finding the tile that is one more or one less, two more or two less than the previously selected tile.

Target pairs

The resources required include: 2–10 digit cards and a tray of Numicon tiles 1–9.

Place the digit cards face down on the table. The child chooses a card, turns it over, and finds two Numicon tiles that add together to make the number on the digit card. If they select correctly, they can keep the digit card and return the Numicon tiles to the tray.

Card and dot games

Spotty six

The resources required include: a dice and a 3 × 3 grid. This is a game for two players. The idea of the game is to make full boxes by drawing a total of six dots in each box. The first player to make a row of three full boxes, horizontally, vertically or diagonally is the winner.

Each player takes turns to roll the dice and to draw that number of dots in one of the boxes on the grid (see Figure 9.5). All of the dots from each throw of the dice must be put into one box. However, you can't have more than six dots in any one box. So, for example, if you throw a five, you can put five dots into an empty box or a box with

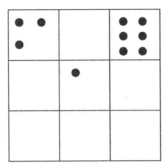

Figure 9.5 Card and dot game

one dot in, but you can't put them into a box with two or more dots as this would entail more than six dots in a box.

This game can be easily modified by varying the number of dots allowed in a box. Or the children can suggest their own ideas for how the game can be varied.

Shut the box

The resources required include: two dice and digit cards 1–12. There is a commercially available version of this game but it can easily be replicated in the classroom using two dice and cards with the numbers 1–12 on them.

Place all the digit cards face up in order from 1 to 12 (ask the learner to do this to check that they are confident in sequencing these numbers). Roll the dice and then turn over the digit cards that match the numbers on the dice or any combination of numbers that add up to the total of the two dice. Thus if the learner rolls a five and a four, they could turn over 9, or 1 and 8, or 2 and 7, or 3 and 6, or 4 and 5, and so on. Play will pass to the next player when a double is thrown. Play continues until a player can't turn over any more cards. Any cards left are added together to give them their score.

You can elect to play a set number of rounds and the player with the lowest score is the winner.

Clear the deck

The resources required include: a deck of cards with the 10s and picture cards removed. This is a game for two players.

Deal out nine cards in a 3 × 3 array, face up for each player. The players then look for pairs of cards that add up to ten and remove them from the table. They then fill those spaces from the remaining cards in the deck. The winner is the first player to clear the deck – that is, there are no cards left in their 3 × 3 array.

Salute!

The resources required include: a pack of playing cards with the picture cards removed. This is a very versatile game for developing number facts. You will need three players for this game.

Two players need to sit opposite each other and the third player sits to the side. Players 1 and 2 both draw a card and place it on their foreheads, without looking at their card: they can see their opponent's card but not their own. The third player calls out what the product of the two cards is. From this call, each player has to work out what card they selected. The first player to give a correct answer keeps both cards and play continues. For each round, the children take it in turns to be the caller.

This game can easily be varied by calling out the sum of the two numbers.

Number bond splat

The resources required include: digit cards 0–9, blue tack, and a 0–9 dice. For this activity, you will need to stick digit cards with numbers from 0 to 9 on the wall.

Decide on a target number and then roll the dice. The idea is to find the number on the wall that will make a bond to the target number. So if the target number is 8 and a 1 is rolled on the dice, the first person to swat the 7 will win that round.

A modification to the above is to choose a target number that is in any times table up to 9 × 9. Then, roll the dice and swat the number that will multiply with the number on the dice to give the target number.

Spotty dog

The resources required include: blank dog templates (see Figure 9.6), counters for the spots, and a 1–6 dice.

Figure 9.6 Spotty dog template

First, roll the dice to see how many dog templates you will have. Roll the dice again to see how many spots to put on each dog. Then work out how many spots there are altogether. Encourage the children to come up with different ways of working out how many spots there are. For example, if you roll 4 and then 5, you will have 4 dogs each with 5 spots on them.

The total number of dots could be 5 + 5 + 5 + 5, or it could be 4 × 5. Or you could work out how many dots there are on two dogs and double the answer.

Other activities to develop number sense

Coincidence or connection

In this activity you can present the child with two related number facts and ask them whether they think the relation is a coincidence or a connection. For example:

5 × 4 = 20
10 × 2 = 20

Is it a coincidence that both products make 20 or is there a connection?

This will help the child to look for connections and to understand the underlying concept more fully. It can help in this example to draw the model for this relationship. For example, the following model represents 5 × 4 = 20 squares:

And the following model represents 10 × 2 = 20 squares:

By showing this array model of multiplication, the child can see that the length has doubled and the width has halved.

Target number

Each day give the children a target number. Their task is to come up with a way of getting to that number. For example, if the target is 12 the child may say 10 + 2 or 6 + 6.

You could vary this and make it more challenging by imposing conditions of asking for multiple solutions. Conditions might include:

- You need to add two numbers.
- You need to add more than two numbers.
- You need to subtract, multiply or divide.
- You need to use at least two different operations.
- You need to use a fraction or a decimal.

The list of conditions is endless and will vary according to the level of learning.

Puppet variation on target number

A fun way of doing the above activity is to use a puppet, preferably a parrot puppet. Explain to the child that this is a very clever puppet, because it can answer mathematical problems. Decide on a target number, say 10 (without revealing this to the child), and then ask the puppet a question to which the answer is ten. Repeat this a couple of times and then ask the child to come up with their own question. Whatever the child asks, the parrot answers ten. The child will soon realize that the parrot can only say ten, so maybe it isn't so clever after all. However, the game now becomes a quest to see how many ways we can come up with questions that have the answer ten, so that we can amaze our friends with how clever our parrot is.

Number grid

For this activity the teacher chooses a number and then asks the child to represent it in four different ways, as illustrated below:

Draw a diagram or picture	Write a number sentence or number story
Write the number as a symbol and as a word	Choose a concrete manipulative to represent the number

This activity can be varied by changing conditions in the boxes according to the level of the learner.

Four 4s

This is a great class activity, as it is a naturally differentiated activity. The idea is that you have to make all of the numbers from 1 to 20 using four 4s and any of the four operations. For example:

$$1 = 4/4 \times 4/4$$
$$2 = 4/4 + 4/4$$

An easy one to work out is:

$$16 = 4 + 4 + 4 + 4$$

Every child in the class will be able to come up with a solution for at least one of the numbers.

NIM games

NIM is a mathematical game of strategy in which two players take turns removing objects from distinct heaps. On each turn, a player must remove at least one object, and may remove any number of objects provided they all come from the same heap. The goal of the game is to be the player to remove the last object.

For NIM-7, place seven counters on the table and decide who is to go first. When subsequent rounds are played, take it in turns to go first. Each player then takes it in turn to take one or two counters from the pile. The player taking the last counter loses. Keep on playing until you have worked out the strategy for winning. Does it matter who goes first?

Activities to develop visualization

Subitizing activities

Subitizing refers to our ability to instantly recognize the number of items in a set without having to count them. Most people can subitize up to 6 or 7 randomly arranged items in a set.

Dyscalculic learners find this very difficult and may not be able to do it at all, even for very small numbers of items. One way that we can help them to develop an appreciation of number magnitude and number sense is to give them opportunities to develop their subitizing ability. For this, we can use dot cards, sometimes referred to as visual cluster cards.

Visual cluster cards

Visual cluster cards are cards with between 0 and 9 dots on them, arranged in different ways (see Figure 9.7). The ways that the dots are arranged can determine what strategies the child uses to work out how many dots are on the card. The idea is for the learner either to instantly recognize how many dots there are on the card or to come up with a visual strategy of working out how many there are without counting them.

This game can be played with a set of visual cluster cards. Whenever the number of dots on a card is given correctly (without one-to-one counting), then the player can keep the card. The player with the

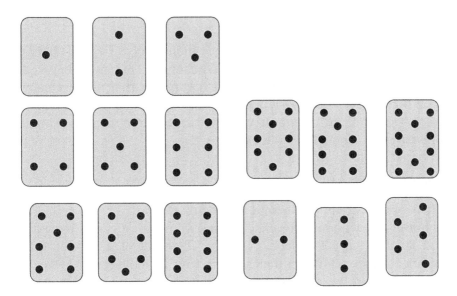

Figure 9.7 Example of visual cluster cards

most cards, or the first player to gain ten cards (depending on the number of players), is the winner.

For example, the two cards shown in Figure 9.8 suggest different ways of 'seeing' the number 7. In the first card, the child may see 7 as a 5 and a 2, because the card shows the dice pattern of 5. In the second card, they may see it as a 4 and a 3, or even two 3s and a 1 at the bottom.

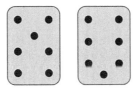

Figure 9.8 Subitizing

Practice with different cards showing different arrangements of dots can really help to develop number sense, how numbers are made, and how they can be broken down. It will also help children to appreciate the magnitude of numbers; for example, understanding that 7 is more than 2 and how many more than 2 it is.

Bunny ears

For this game the players need to use their fingers to make bunny ears on each side of their head. The teacher calls out a number from 2 to 10 and the children then need to represent that number using their fingers. For example, if you call 6 the children could use 5 fingers from one hand and 1 finger from the other, or three from each hand, or 4 from one and 2 from the other.

What am I hiding?

The resources required include: multi-link cubes.

   Both the teacher and the child join a set number of cubes to make a rod of cubes, say a rod made of 9 cubes. Then each player breaks off a number of cubes and hides them in their hand. By looking at the remaining cubes, the other player has to work out how many cubes they are hiding. In this case, with a rod of 9, if I can see that my opponent has 5 cubes left in their rod, then they must be hiding 4 in their hand.

Finger discrimination activities

In this activity, students place coloured dots on their fingers and then the teacher asks them to touch the corresponding piano keys, as shown in Figure 9.9.

Activities to develop place value

Ten exchange

The resources required include: a bag of 100 unit cubes and 10 rods.

   Ask the child to grab a few handfuls of unit cubes and throw them onto the table. Can they estimate how many cubes are there? Now, sort the cubes into groups of ten and exchange them for ten rods. Can they now tell you exactly how many cubes there are? Is their estimate close?

Nice or nasty game

The resources required include: a 0–9 dice or spinner and paper and pencils. For each player, draw a play grid, as shown in Figure 9.10.

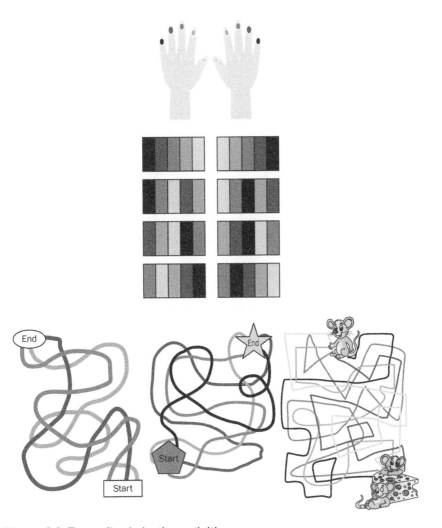

Figure 9.9 Finger discrimination activities

Figure 9.10 Play grid for the nice or nasty game

Nice game. The aim is to make the largest number you can from rolling the dice four times. On each roll you will need to decide where on the grid to place that number in order to give you the largest number.

You can score a point in two ways:

- Simply by scoring a point for each win and then the first person to reach 5 points is the winner.
- Or, for a more advanced level, you can calculate the difference between the two numbers and the winner keeps that score. The first person to reach a score of 10,000 is the winner.

Variations to the above include the winner having to make the smallest four-digit number. You can change the playing grid, for example, by adding two three-digit numbers to make the smallest or largest four-digit number. You could also introduce variations involving subtraction or multiplication. There are endless possibilities!

Nasty game. You can play any of the versions of the game detailed above, but this time you roll the dice and put the number in your opponent's grid to try and make sure that they don't win. So if you are looking for the largest four-digit number and you roll a 9, then you would put this in the ones place in your opponent's grid.

The bar model

The bar model is a very effective way of solving word problems. It acts as a bridge between the word problem and the actual calculation that needs to be carried out to solve that problem. Word problems are notoriously difficult for learners who struggle with maths and this approach really helps them to 'see' what they need to do. The examples that are illustrated here are drawn from the Singapore Ministry for Education book, *The Singapore Model Method for Learning Mathematics* (Hong et al. 2009).

There are three different types of model:

1. the part–whole model
2. the comparison model
3. the change model.

The part–whole model. Initially, the part–whole model is used to represent simple addition problems. For example:

> Jack has 4 biscuits and Sam has 7 biscuits. How many biscuits do they have altogether?

This problem can be modelled with real objects, then with cubes to represent the objects followed by abstract representation using bars. The two quantities are added together, giving 4 + 7 = 11. This problem may be represented pictorially as shown in Figure 9.11.

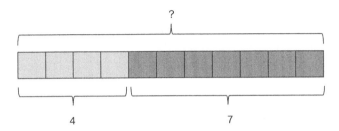

This can also be visualized as two parts making a whole:

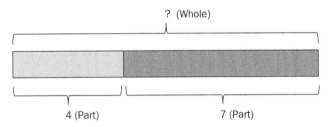

Figure 9.11 Part–whole model

The comparison model. In this model, two quantities are compared. For example, in a group of children there are 5 more boys than girls. If there are 10 girls, then how many boys are there? This can be modelled using bars as shown in Figure 9.12.

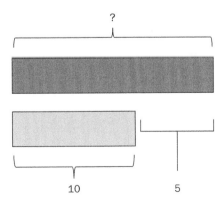

Figure 9.12 Comparison model

The change model

In change model problems, there are two models: one for the situation before the change and one for the situation after the change. For example:

> Aran has five times as much money as Abigail. Aran gives Abigail £10 and now they both have the same amount. How much money did Aran have to begin with?

Before model. Aran must have given two parts to Abigail for them to have the same amount at the end. Each part must therefore be 5 (see Figure 9.13).

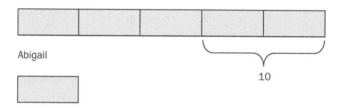

Figure 9.13 Before model

After model. So at the beginning, Aran must have had £25 (see Figure 9.14).

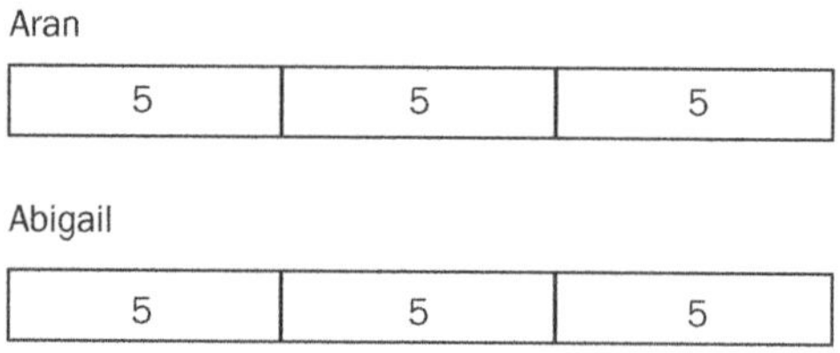

Aran

5	5	5

Abigail

5	5	5

Figure 9.14 After model

References

Dienes, Z. (1969) *Building up Mathematics*. London: Hutchinson Education.

Gattegno, C. and Cuisenaire, G. (1954) *Numbers in Colour*. London: Heinemann.

Hong, K.T., Mei, Y.S. and Lim, J. (2009) *The Singapore Model Method for Learning Mathematics*. Singapore: EPB Pan Pacific.

Papert, S. (1980) *Mindstorms: Children, computers and powerful ideas*. New York: Basic Books.

Piaget, J. (1952) *The Child's Conception of Number*. New York: Humanities Press.

Stein, M. and Bovalino, J. (2001) Manipulatives: one piece of the puzzle, *Mathematics Teaching in the Middle School*, 6(6): 356–60.

10 Curiosity

> It is magic until you understand it and it is mathematics thereafter.
>
> > Bharati Krishna

> Mathematics has beauty and romance. It's not a boring place to be, the mathematical world. It's an extraordinary place; it's worth spending time there.
>
> > Marcus du Sautoy (2006)

Dyscalculic learners will find maths a struggle, and one of the battles that we as educators have is keeping them interested in maths and motivating them to keep on going when things get tough. Gelman et al. conducted research to explore how curiosity influences memory. They found that there was a link 'between the mechanisms supporting extrinsic reward motivation and intrinsic curiosity' and that this highlights 'the importance of stimulating curiosity to create more effective learning experiences' (2014: 486).

So this chapter is here to provide you with some of the 'Wow!' moments in maths. They are a few of my favourite activities and have re-energized many a flagging learner in the past. I hope that you enjoy them as much as I and my learners do.

Magic squares

Magic squares hold a fascination for many a mathematician. In a basic magic square, the rows, columns, and two diagonals all add up to the same number. This is called the magic number and in Figure 10.1 the magic number is 15.

8	1	6
3	5	7
4	9	2

Figure 10.1 Magic square

There are examples of more complex magic squares and the one illustrated in Figure 10.2 is from the legendary mathematician Srinivasa Ramanujan. He created a much more complex magic square where not only do the rows and columns add to the same total, 139, but there are also many other patterns, as shown in Figure 10.3. Can you find any others?

22	12	18	87
88	17	9	25
10	24	89	16
19	86	23	11

Figure 10.2 More complex magic square

22	12	18	87		22	12	18	87
88	17	9	25		88	17	9	25
10	24	89	16		10	24	89	16
14	86	23	11		19	86	23	11

Figure 10.3 Other patterns in a magic square

It is also worthy of note that the top row is Ramanujan's date of birth: 22 December 1887.

Sagrada Familia

One of my favourite magic squares can be found in Barcelona at the Sagrada Familia, shown in Figure 10.4. It also has many different patterns to explore. The magic number here is 33, which was the age that Jesus was when he was crucified. There are dozens of combinations of numbers that would produce a similar square, with numbers adding to 33.

1	14	14	4
11	7	6	9
8	10	10	5
13	2	3	15

Figure 10.4 Magic square from Sagrada Familia

How to construct a magic square

In the nineteenth century, Edouard Lucas devised the general formula for order 3 magic squares. Consider the following table made up of numbers a, b, and c.

$c - b$	$c + (a + b)$	$c - a$
$c - (a - b)$	c	$c + (a - b)$
$c + a$	$c - (a + b)$	$c + b$

These numbers will form a magic square so long as:

1   they are all larger than zero
2   b must be larger than a
3   b must not be the same value as 2 times a
4   c – a must be bigger than both a and b.

What's so special about 2016?

Can we use the numbers 1 to 10 and the four number operations to make 2016? Yes, indeed we can. Here are two examples:

$$\frac{10 \times 9 \times 8 \times 7 \times 6}{5 + 4 + 3 + 2 + 1}$$

$$3^3 + 4^3 + 5^3 + 6^3 + 7^3 + 8^3 + 9^3 = 2016$$

The golden ratio

The golden ratio, denoted by the Greek symbol 'phi', is a special number in maths that is approximately equal to 1.618. It appears in many areas of life such as architecture, art and geometry, and even in the human body (see Figure 10.5).

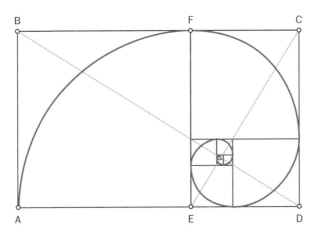

Figure 10.5 The golden ratio

The golden ratio is found by dividing a line into two unequal parts so that the whole length of the line divided by the longer part is equal to the longer part divided by the shorter part. Try exploring this yourself!

$$\frac{a+b}{a} = \frac{a}{b} = 1.618\ldots = \varphi$$

As humans, we like to see objects around us that are in the golden ratio, such as picture frames. The proportions of many buildings are also designed to be in the golden ratio.

The golden ratio and the Fibonacci sequence

There is a special relationship between the golden ratio and the Fibonacci sequence. The Fibonacci sequence is as follows:

0, 1, 1, 2, 3, 5, 8, 13, 21, 34 . . .

The sequence starts with 0, 1, and then the next number is found by adding up the two numbers that precede it – so, 0 + 1 = 1.

The relationship between the golden ratio and the Fibonacci sequence is that the ratio of two consecutive numbers from the sequence is very close to the golden ratio and gets closer the further along the sequence that you go.

Everlasting chocolate

The everlasting chocolate trick appears to make a square of chocolate appear out of nowhere. Clearly, this is an attractive thought for even the most reluctant mathematician!

There are several YouTube clips that both illustrate and explain this phenomenon.

A couple of the better ones are:

- https://www.youtube.com/watch?v=dmBsPgPu0Wc
- https://www.youtube.com/watch?v=ltqHJTY8Fhk

Vedic maths

Vedic maths is based on 16 sutras or principles. These principles are general in nature and can be applied in many ways. In practice, many applications of the sutras may be learned and combined to solve actual problems. The following examples of simple applications of the sutras give a feel for how the Vedic maths system works.

Multiplying by 11

This is a way of quickly calculating the answer when a number is multiplied by 11. For example:

$$26 \times 11 = 286$$

One can work this answer out by adding the 2 and 6 from 26, which equals 8, and putting that number between the 2 and the 6:

$$2\ 8\ 6 = 286$$

This works when the two digits add to a number less than 10. If they add to a number that is 10 or more, then you have to make the following adjustment:

$$48 \times 11 = 4\ ([4 + 8 =]\ 12)\ 8$$

In this case we would have 4128, which would be incorrect, so we need to take the 1 and add it to the first digit, giving 528, which is the correct solution.

Try a few for yourself.

Dividing by 9

$$24/9 = 2 \text{ remainder } 6$$

The first number is how many 9s there are in 24 and the remainder is the two digits added together:

$$24/9 = 2 \text{ remainder } (2 + 4) = 2 \text{ remainder } 6$$

Adding periods of time

To add two periods of time together, you simply write the times as three-digit numbers, add them together, and then add 40. For example:

1 hour and 35 minutes plus 2 hours and 55 minutes
$$= 135 + 255 + 40$$
$$= 430$$
$$= 4 \text{ hours and } 30 \text{ minutes!}$$

Three-digit trick

1 Write down any three-digit number
2 Multiply it by 13
3 Multiply that figure by 7
4 And, finally, multiply that answer by 11

What do you notice? Does it always work? Why?

Nomography

I have read many maths books and come across many interesting maths things, but this one I found to be truly astounding. It is all to do with a branch of maths called nomenclature. In this example, we are going to use the graph of $y = x^2$ to help us to multiply two numbers. For example, if we want to multiply 5 by 8:

1   Plot the graph of $y = x^2$
2   Draw a line that crosses the parabola where $x = -5$ and where $x = 8$ on the parabola (don't worry that we are using –5 instead of 5).
3   Note the value of y where the line crosses the y-axis.

The value of y is 40 and indeed $5 \times 8 = 40$ as shown in Figure 10.6.

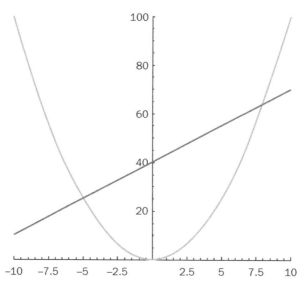

Figure 10.6 Nomography

Escher tessellations

Maurits Cornelis Escher was one of the world's most famous graphic artists. He loved creating tessellations (see Figure 10.7) which are shapes that fit together to fill the whole of a plane space. The instructions in Figure 10.8 will enable you to create your own Escher tessellation.

Figure 10.7 Escher tessellations

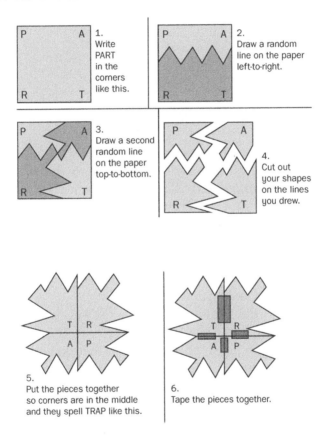

Figure 10.8 Create your own Escher tessellations

More information and examples of Escher's work can be found at: www.mcescher.com.

Mobius strip

This is my all-time favourite activity to do with learners of any age and with the teachers that I work with too. The Mobius strip (see Figure 10.9) is named after the mathematician August Mobius who invented the strip in 1858. It is curious because it only has one side and one edge. A Mobius strip is simple to construct. All you need is a long strip of paper, sticky tape and a pair of scissors.

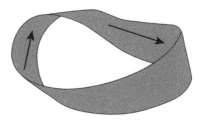

Figure 10.9 Mobius strip

Take the long piece of paper and put the ends together as if you were making a headband. Before you attach the two ends with tape, give one of them a twist and then stick the ends together. Now try drawing a line along the centre of the strip. What do you notice?

You will end up back where you started, without having to take your pen off the paper. So you have drawn on both sides of the strip of paper in one go, meaning that your original strip of paper, which had two sides, now only has one side!

Now cut along the line that you have drawn. What do you think might happen? Try it and see!

There are many other interesting things that you can do with this strip. Try making another one, but this time instead of cutting along the middle, cut a third of the way from one edge. What do you think will happen this time?

References

du Sautoy, M. (2006) A prime example, *The Guardian*, 19 December [retrieved from: https://www.theguardian.com/education/2006/dec/19/academicexperts.highereducationprofile; accessed 19 March 2017].

Gelman, B., Gruber, M. and Ranganath, C. (2014) States of curiosity modulate hippocampus-dependent learning via the dopaminergic circuit, *Neuron*, 84(2): 486–96.

Useful websites

www.stevechinn.co.uk
www.mathematicalbrain.com
www.bda-dyslexia.org.uk
www.dyscalculia.org.uk
www.dyscalculia.me.uk
www.dyscalculia-maths-difficulties.org.uk
www.ronitbird.co.uk
www.aboutdyscalculia.org
www.judyhornigold.co.uk
www.nrich.maths.org
www.dynamomaths.co.uk
www.dyscalculia-maths-difficulties.org.uk

Book resources

The Trouble with Maths: A practical guide to helping learners with numeracy difficulties by Steve Chinn (2017) 3rd Edition. Abingdon: Routledge.

Making Maths Visual and Tactile by Judy Hornigold (2016) Wakefield: SEN Books.

More Trouble with Maths: A complete guide to identifying and diagnosing mathematical difficulties by Steve Chinn (2017) 2nd Edition. Abingdon: Routledge.

Dyscalculia Guidance: Helping pupils with specific learning difficulties in maths by Brian Butterworth and Dorian Yeo (2004) Slough: NFER/Nelson.

Dyscalculia Lesson Plans Books 1 and 2 by Judy Hornigold (2014) Nottingham: TTS.

Dyscalculia Pocketbook by Judy Hornigold (2015) Alresford: Teachers' Pocketbooks.

The Dyscalculia Assessment by Jane Emerson and Patricia Babtie (2013) London: Bloomsbury.

The Dyscalculia Solution by Jane Emerson and Patricia Babtie (2014) London: Bloomsbury.

Mathematics for Dyslexics and Dyscalculics. A teaching handbook 4th edn. Chichester, Wiley, Chinn, S. and Ashcroft, R. (2017).

Dyscalculia Toolkit: Supporting learning difficulties in maths by Ronit Bird (2013) London: Sage.

The Dyscalculia Resource Book by Ronit Bird (2011) London: Sage.

The Routledge International Handbook of Dyscalculia and Mathematical Learning Difficulties by Steve Chinn (2015) Abingdon: Routledge.

Understanding Dyscalculia and Numeracy Difficulties by Patricia Babtie and Jane Emerson (2015) London: Jessica Kingsley Publishers.

Appendix

List of suitable tests for specific learning difficulties in maths

Category	Name of test	Age range	Admin time	Components	Comments
Underlying ability	Wide Range Intelligence Test (WRIT)	4–85 years	20–30 min	Verbal (Vocabulary & Verbal Analogies); Visual (Matrices & Diamonds)	High correlation with WAIS-III and WISC-III; co-normed with WRAT3. Published 2000
Working memory	Wide Range Assessment of Memory and Learning, Second Edition (WRAML-2)	5–90 years	20+ min	6 core tests; 2 optional delay recall tests; 4 optional recognition tests; 3 optional memory tests	The factor structure contains verbal memory, visual memory, and attention/concentration information. Excellent range of memory tests
	The digit memory test	6 years–adult	5–10 min	Digit span forward and backward	
Phonological processing	Comprehensive Test of Phonological Processing (CTOPP)	5–24 years 11 months	30 min	Phonological Awareness Quotient; Phonological Memory Quotient; Rapid Naming Quotient; Alternative Phonological Awareness Quotient; Alternative Rapid Naming Quotient	Can be used qualitatively for ages over 24 years and 11 months
Speed of processing	Symbol Digit Modalities Test (SDMT)	8 years–adult	90 sec	Matching number with symbol	
	Comprehensive Test of Phonological Processing (CTOPP)	5–24 years 11 months	30 min	All Rapid Naming Subtests and Quotients	

(Continued)

Appendix (*continued*)

Category	Name of test	Age range	Admin time	Components	Comments
Numeracy	WRAT-Expanded Individual Assessment (Form I) Mathematics Test	7–24 years 11 months	15 min		Multiple-choice; assesses understanding of concepts, computation, and problem-solving. Can be used qualitatively for ages over 24 years 11 months
	WRAT 4 Maths Competency Test	7–75 years 11 1/2 years–adult	30 min 30–40 min	Numeracy Using & Applying Mathematics; Number & Algebra; Space & Shape; Handling Data	Useful for students who have difficulty with mathematics; gives percentile scores only; can be used qualitatively
	Basic Number test Sandwell	7–12 years 4–8 years	Not timed 10–30 min	Assesses basic number skills Five strands of basic numeracy skills: identification, oral counting, value, object counting, and language	One-to-one
	Sandwell	8–14 years	10–30 min	Five strands of basic numeracy skills: identification, oral counting, value, object counting, and language	One-to-one
	Key Maths 3	6–16 years 11 months	30–90 min	Basic Concepts (conceptual knowledge), Operations (computational skills), and Applications (problem-solving)	One-to-one

Index

ESSENTIAL PRIMARY MATHEMATICS

Rickard

ISBN: 9780335247028 (Paperback)
eISBN: 9780335247035

2013

If you are teaching or learning to teach primary mathematics, this is the toolkit to support you! Not only does it cover the essential knowledge and understanding that you and your pupils need to know, it also offers 176 great ideas for teaching primary mathematics - adaptable for use within different areas of mathematics and for different ages and abilities.

- Think deeply about mathematics and to challenge themselves
- Develop mathematical independence
- Engage in mathematical talk

www.mheducation.co.uk